Simple Double-Dipped Quilts

SCRAPPY QUILTS BUILT FROM BLOCKS WITH A UNIQUE TWIST

KIM DIEHL

Martingale®
Create with Confidence

Simple Double-Dipped Quilts:
Scrappy Quilts Built from Blocks with a Unique Twist
© 2022 by Kim Diehl

Martingale®
18939 120th Ave NE, Suite 101
Bothell, WA 98011-9511 USA
ShopMartingale.com

No part of this product may be reproduced in any form, unless otherwise stated, in which case reproduction is limited to the use of the purchaser. The written instructions, photographs, designs, projects, and patterns are intended for the personal, noncommercial use of the retail purchaser and are under federal copyright laws; they are not to be reproduced by any electronic, mechanical, or other means, including informational storage or retrieval systems, for commercial use. Permission is granted to photocopy patterns for the personal use of the retail purchaser. Attention teachers: Martingale encourages you to use this book for teaching, subject to the restrictions stated above.

The information in this book is presented in good faith, but no warranty is given nor results guaranteed. Since Martingale has no control over choice of materials or procedures, the company assumes no responsibility for the use of this information.

Printed in the United States of America
27 26 25 24 23 22   8 7 6 5 4 3 2 1

Library of Congress Cataloging-in-Publication Data is available upon request.

ISBN: 978-1-68356-228-3

MISSION STATEMENT

We empower makers who use fabric and yarn to make life more enjoyable.

CREDITS

**PRESIDENT AND
CHIEF VISIONARY OFFICER**
Jennifer Erbe Keltner

CONTENT DIRECTOR
Karen Costello Soltys

DESIGN MANAGER
Adrienne Smitke

COPY EDITOR
Sheila Chapman Ryan

PRODUCTION MANAGER
Regina Girard

ILLUSTRATOR
Sandy Loi

PHOTOGRAPHERS
Adam Albright
Brent Kane

SPECIAL THANKS
Some of the photography for this book was taken at the home of Samantha Keltner in Des Moines, Iowa, and at Lori Clarke's Little Farmhouse in Snohomish, Washington.

Contents

Introduction

For many years I've been stitching together scraps of fabric while blending blocks, merging motifs, and tweaking the traditional. Without even realizing it, I was "double dipping" many of my quilts.

If you're wondering what double dipping is, please let me tell you that no, it doesn't mean going in for that second scoop of guacamole on the sly! Double dipping is my term for taking a tried-and-true quilt block, or a classic motif that's been loved by generations of quilters, and adding an unexpected surprise or twist to make it unique.

As you explore the projects in this book, you'll find a sampling of 10 thoroughly fun-to-stitch quilts that each began with a conventional block, a bit of imagination, and the tiny seed of an idea. These quilts range from bed size to mini, from patchwork to appliqué, and there are lots of scrappy color schemes guaranteed to make you want to dive into your stash or stock up on new prints at your favorite quilt shop. Or heck, do both! You shouldn't have to choose!

In the spirit of "double your pleasure, double your fun," each project features a Double-Take tip for added inspiration. This means that for every quilt there are bonus ideas such as alternate settings, simple patchwork tweaks to easily change things up, or different color-scheme options for a whole different vibe. Watch for these double takes, because they basically give you an arsenal of extra tricks up your sleeve to *double* the possibilities for your 10 quilts.

Have I piqued your interest? I sure hope so, because my goal is to spark your imagination, encourage you to stitch, and cheer you on as you answer the call of your sewing room!

~ *Kim*

Just Passing Through

When does a basic Flying Geese block become something beyond basic? When you double dip it and transform it into a show-off block with a surprise patchwork center! Colorful checkerboard squares add homey charm peeking out from the middle of selected blocks, and a flock of star silhouettes scattered across the top adds just the right touch of twinkle.

FINISHED QUILT SIZE: 60½" × 70½" | **FINISHED BLOCK SIZE: 5" × 10"**

MATERIALS

Yardage is based on a 42" width of useable fabric after prewashing and removing selvages.

32 chubby sixteenths (9" × 10½") of assorted prints for checkerboard patchwork

22 fat quarters (18" × 21") of assorted dark prints divided into groups:

- 12 for cream-centered blocks
- 7 for star units
- 3 for dark-centered blocks

⅞ yard *each* of 6 assorted cream prints for Flying Geese blocks*

¾ yard of black print for stars and binding

3¾ yards of fabric for backing

67" × 77" rectangle of batting

*See cutting instructions for the cream prints on page 8; if you don't prewash your fabrics, you may be able reduce the amount of each cream print to ¾ yard.

CUTTING

Cut all pieces across the width of the fabric in the order given unless otherwise noted.

From *each* of the 32 assorted chubby sixteenths, cut:
5 strips, 1½" × 10½" (combined total of 160).
Note: For even scrappier checkerboard units, cut some of these strips from scraps in your stash.

From *each* of the 6 cream prints, cut:
5 strips, 5½" × 42"; crosscut into:
- 12 squares, 5½" × 5½" (combined total of 72)
- 8 rectangles, 5½" × 10½" (combined total of 48)
  Note: If you haven't prewashed your fabrics you may be able to cut 8 rectangles, 5½" × 10½", from 2 strips, and reduce the total number of strips needed to 4.

From *each of 12* fat quarters of assorted dark prints for cream-centered Flying Geese blocks, cut:
3 strips, 5½" × 21"; crosscut into 8 squares, 5½" × 5½" (combined total of 96)

From *each of the 7* fat quarters for the star units, cut:
1 rectangle, 5½" × 10½" (combined total of 7)
4 rectangles, 2½" × 4½" (combined total of 28)
1 square, 2½" × 2½" (combined total of 7)
2 rectangles, 1½" × 4½" (combined total of 14)
1 rectangle, 1½" × 2½" (combined total of 7)
Add the 5½" × 10½" rectangles to the dark-centered Flying Geese pieces below. Group the remaining pieces by matching prints into star-background sets.

From the 3 fat quarters of assorted prints for dark-centered Flying Geese blocks, cut *a combined total* of:
7 rectangles, 5½" × 10½"

From the black print, cut:
1 strip, 2½" × 42"; crosscut into 7 squares, 2½" × 2½".
  From the remainder of this strip, cut 4 squares, 1½" × 1½".
2 strips, 1½" × 42"; crosscut into 52 squares, 1½" × 1½" (combined total of 56 with previously cut squares)
7 binding strips, 2½" × 42" (For my chubby-binding method on page 103, reduce the strip width to 2".)

PIECING THE CHECKERBOARD FLYING GEESE BLOCKS

Sew all pieces with right sides together using a ¼" seam allowance unless otherwise noted. Press the seam allowances as indicated by the arrows or as otherwise specified. Before beginning, I found it helpful to divide the strips into two piles—one of lighter prints and one of darker prints. This organizational step is entirely up to you!

1. Choose two 1½" × 10½" strips, one lighter print and one darker. (Keep in mind that the light and dark values of any given print can change, depending upon the print it's paired with.) Join the pair of strips along the long edges. Press. Repeat with the remaining strips, each time joining a lighter and a darker print and pressing toward the darker print, until all of the strips have been sewn into pairs.

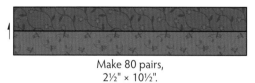

Make 80 pairs,
2½" × 10½".

2. Select five sewn pairs of strips. Rotate the direction of every other pair 180° so the prints roughly alternate between light and dark. Join the pairs together along the long edges. Press, again directing the seam allowances toward the darker prints. (Pressing the seam allowances toward the darker prints will help them nest together when the checkerboard units are pieced.) Continue adding strip pairs until you have joined 10 strips for a strip set measuring 10½" square, including the seam allowances. Repeat to make a total of 16 strip sets.

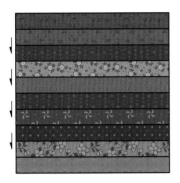

Make 16 strip sets,
10½" × 10½".

3. Crosscut each strip set at 1½" intervals to yield six segments, 1½" × 10½"; you'll have 96 pieced segments. Keep the segments cut from each strip set organized into a separate pile so you easily see your choices as you piece the checkerboard units.

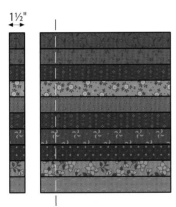

Cut 6 segments,
1½" × 10½".

4. Lay out five assorted segments in five horizontal rows, turning the direction of every other row 180° so the light and dark prints roughly alternate and the seams will nest together. Join the rows. Press. Repeat to piece a total of 15 checkerboard units measuring 5½" × 10½", including the seam allowances. (You'll

Pin Point Tip

SKINNY SEAMS

Experience has taught me that even when using an accurate ¼" seam allowance, patchwork units such as a checkerboard can finish slightly smaller than our calculations, simply because of the number of seams and the tiny bit of cloth that's lost to the fold of each one. To compensate, I routinely stitch these types of projects using "skinny" seams, meaning two or three threads less than a true ¼".

As an added safety measure before beginning a new project that will benefit from skinny seams, I sew a quick test piece using four or five scrap patches in the needed size. When sewing, I adjust the width of the seams and pay careful attention to the placement of the patchwork, noting how it rests against the guide of the ¼" sewing-machine foot.

After pressing the seam allowances as instructed in the project directions, I measure and evaluate the results of the finished inner strips (not the strips with raw edges on the outer edges of the unit) to see if my piecing is spot on, or if I need to make further adjustments. With this step under my belt, I can confidently dive into my project at full speed, taking care to duplicate the placement of my patchwork under the presser foot as it was in my test, knowing that my accuracy will help the remainder of the project come together easily.

have a handful of leftover strip-set segments; these have been included for added choices as you piece the checkerboard units.)

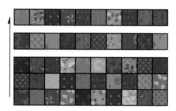

Make 15 checkerboard units,
5½" × 10½".

5. Use a pencil and an acrylic ruler to draw a diagonal sewing line from corner to corner on the wrong side of the 72 assorted cream print 5½" squares.

6. Choose two matching-print prepared cream 5½" squares. Layer a prepared square onto one end of a step 4 checkerboard unit as shown, right. Stitch along the drawn diagonal line. Fold the resulting inner triangle open, aligning the corner with the corner of the checkerboard unit. Press. Trim away the layers beneath the top cream triangle, leaving a ¼" seam allowance. In the same manner, add a mirror-image cream triangle corner to the remaining end of the

checkerboard unit using the matching cream square. Repeat to piece a total of 15 Checkerboard Flying Geese blocks measuring 5½" × 10½", including the seam allowances. Reserve the remaining prepared cream 5½" squares for later use.

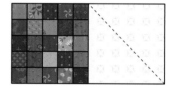

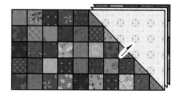

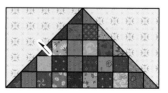

Make 15 Checkerboard Flying Geese blocks,
5½" × 10½".

Simple Double-Dipped Quilts

Pin Point Tip

BONUS CHECKERBOARD PATCHWORK UNITS

For zero waste when stitching Checkerboard Flying Geese blocks, try this approach as you're piecing the blocks. You'll also end up with a tidy little pile of bonus checkerboard patchwork units!

In addition to stitching along the drawn diagonal line on each prepared 5½" cream square, stitch a second seam ½" away from the first line of stitching, closer to the outer corner of the unit. Once both seams have been sewn, cut the patchwork apart between the two sewn lines, leaving a ¼" seam allowance on each unit. Press the seam allowance of the resulting bonus checkerboard unit toward the cream print and square it up to whatever size you'd like. These sweet little checkerboard half-square-triangle units can be used to make throw pillows, a bonus mini quilt, or any creative project you can imagine!

PIECING THE STAR FLYING GEESE BLOCKS

1. Draw a diagonal sewing line on the wrong side of each black 1½" square as previously instructed.

2. Layer a prepared black 1½" square onto the bottom-right corner of a 2½" × 4½" print rectangle, right sides together. Stitch, press, and trim as instructed in step 6 of the Checkerboard Flying Geese blocks on page 10. In the same manner stitch a second black 1½" square to the top-right corner of the rectangle to make a side star-point unit. Repeat to piece two side star-point units measuring 2½" × 4½", including the seam allowances.

Make 2 side
star-point units,
2½" × 4½".

3. Use two prepared black 1½" squares and one print 2½" square to piece one top star-point unit measuring 2½" square, including the seam allowances.

Make 1 top unit,
2½" × 2½".

4. Using two prepared black 1½" squares and a print 1½" × 2½" rectangle, piece one bottom star-point unit measuring 1½" × 2½", including the seam allowances.

Make 1 bottom unit,
1½" × 2½".

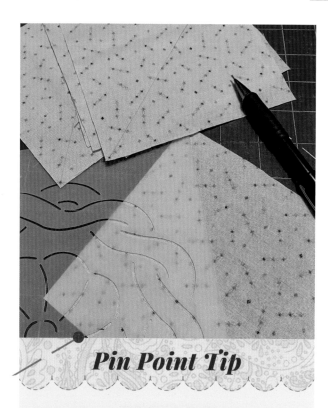

Pin Point Tip

ACRYLIC RULER ALTERNATIVE

When I'm marking diagonal sewing lines on larger squares such as those called for in this project, I find that the bigger acrylic rulers needed can sometimes feel awkward and bulky. An easy-to-use alternative is to grab a quilting stencil made from template plastic, or even just use a whole square of clear template plastic in a size that fits the patchwork pieces. Because the plastic's transparent and lightweight, it's easy to align a side of the template with the corners of the square without a lot of maneuvering to correctly position it, and there's just enough of a raised edge to easily be able to run your pencil along the side to mark the sewing line. This little trick is a great time-saver and makes it a snap to prep patchwork pieces.

5. Lay out the four star-point units, the two print 2½" × 4½" rectangles, the two print 1½" × 4½" rectangles, and the black 2½" square in three horizontal rows as shown. Join the pieces in each row. Press. Join the rows. Press. The pieced star unit should measure 5½" × 10½", including the seam allowances.

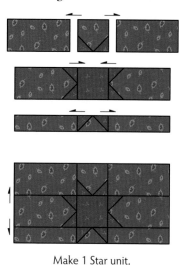

Make 1 Star unit,
5½" × 10½".

6. Use two reserved prepared cream 5½" squares to add stitch-and-fold triangle corners to the star unit as for the Checkerboard Flying Geese blocks.

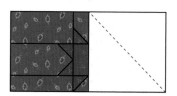

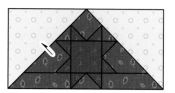

Make 1 Star Flying Geese block,
5½" × 10½".

Simple Double-Dipped Quilts

Designed and pieced by Kim Diehl. Machine quilted by Connie Tabor.

7. Repeat steps 2–6 to piece a total of seven Star Flying Geese blocks measuring 5½" × 10½", including seam allowances. Reserve the remaining prepared cream 5½" squares for the dark-centered Flying Geese blocks.

PIECING THE DARK- AND LIGHT-CENTERED FLYING GEESE BLOCKS

1. For each dark-centered Flying Geese block select one print 5½" × 10½" rectangle (hereafter referred to as "dark") and two matching reserved prepared cream 5½" squares. Use the cream squares to sew a stitch-and-fold corner to each end of the dark rectangle as previously instructed. Repeat to piece a total of 14 dark-centered Flying Geese blocks measuring 5½" × 10½", including the seam allowances.

2. Draw a diagonal sewing line on the wrong side of each assorted print 5½" square (hereafter referred to as "dark") as previously instructed.

3. Select two matching prepared dark 5½" squares and one cream 5½" × 10½" rectangle. Use the two squares to sew a stitch-and-fold triangle to each end of the cream rectangle as previously instructed. Repeat to piece 48 light-centered Flying Geese blocks measuring 5½" × 10½", including the seam allowances.

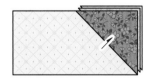

Make 48 cream-centered blocks,
5½" × 10½".

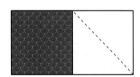

Make 14 dark-centered blocks,
5½" × 10½".

PIECING THE QUILT TOP

Referring to the quilt assembly diagram, right, lay out all styles of the Flying Geese blocks in 12 horizontal rows of seven blocks each. Join the blocks in each horizontal row. Press. Join the rows. Press. The pieced quilt top should measure 60½" × 70½".

COMPLETING THE QUILT

Layer and baste the quilt top, batting, and backing. Quilt the layers. The featured quilt is machine quilted with an edge-to-edge design of repeating and echo-quilted curved triangular shapes to add movement to the straight lines of the patchwork. Join the black binding strips to make one length and use it to bind the quilt.

Quilt assembly

Double-Take Tip

LIFTING OFF? OR LANDING?

For a super quick and easy alternate layout that subtly changes the feel of the featured quilt, try turning the direction of the even-numbered columns, rotating them 180° to position the points downward. Modifying the direction of these blocks and reorienting the points of the flying geese is an easy change, and it brings an even greater sense of movement to the quilt design.

Alternate layout

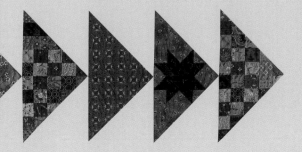

Hope and Harmony

Having seen so many different layouts and approaches to the classic clamshell during my years as a quilter, I wondered, could it be double dipped to put an entirely new spin on it? You bet it could! The addition of simple but plentiful almond-shaped leaves completely transforms the clamshell, and suddenly it's not the just the shell of a shape, but a blossom in full bloom.

FINISHED QUILT SIZE: 60½" × 63½" | **FINISHED BLOCK SIZE: 10" × 9"**

MATERIALS

Yardage is based on a 42" width of useable fabric after prewashing and removing selvages.

⅔ yard *each* of 6 assorted cream prints for block backgrounds

42 chubby sixteenths (9" × 10½") of assorted medium and dark prints for appliqués and binding*

3¾ yards of fabric for backing

67" × 70" rectangle of batting

Supplies for your favorite appliqué method, including freezer paper for making a pattern template

Liquid seam sealant (such as Fray Check) is optional but recommended

* If you have a large stash, you can draw from your scraps and include even more prints for greater variety. For a more planned look using fewer prints, you can swap 21 fat eighths for the 42 chubby sixteenths.

CUTTING

Cut all pieces across the width of the fabric in the order given unless otherwise noted. Instructions for cutting the appliqués are provided separately in step 2, right.

From *each* of the 6 assorted cream prints, cut:
2 strips, 10½" × 42"; crosscut into 7 rectangles, 10½" × 9½" (combined total of 42)

From 32 of the medium and dark prints, cut:
1 strip, 2½" × 9", for binding. Reserve the remainder of these prints for cutting appliqués.

CUTTING AND APPLIQUÉING THE CLAMSHELL BLOSSOM BLOCKS

The clamshell and leaf appliqué patterns are provided on page 23. Use freezer paper and refer to "Preparing Pattern Tracing Templates" on page 97 to make a pattern tracing template for the steps that follow, or substitute your own favorite method.

1. I recommend applying a thin line of liquid seam sealant around the edges of each cream rectangle to protect them from fraying as you handle them during the appliqué steps, but this is entirely up to you. Fold each rectangle in half vertically, right sides together, and use a hot, dry iron to lightly press a center crease.

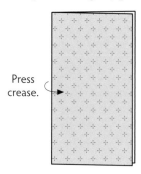

Press crease.

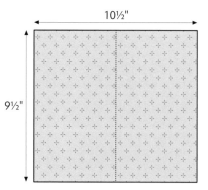

10½"

9½"

2. Using the reserved remainder of the 42 assorted medium and dark prints, the prepared tracing templates, and your favorite appliqué method (my invisible machine-appliqué preparation steps begin on page 97, if you'd like to use this method), cut and prepare:

- 1 clamshell appliqué from each of the 42 assorted prints (combined total of 42)
- 13 leaf appliqués from each of the 42 assorted prints (combined total of 546). You can include additional prints from your stash if you'd like even greater variety.

Please note that you can position the appliqué templates on the fabric in any direction you'd like to take best advantage of your prints and the size of your scraps.

3. Choose a prepared cream rectangle, one clamshell appliqué, and 13 assorted print leaf appliqués. Fold the top of the clamshell appliqué in half vertically, with right sides together, and finger-press a short crease at the top edge. Align the clamshell's top crease with the crease of the block background, positioning the clamshell's narrow bottom end over the crease at the bottom of the block, raw edges flush, to center the appliqué. Pin or baste the clamshell in place, or use my appliqué glue-basting technique described on page 100.

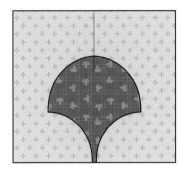

Position and baste the clamshell.

4. Position and baste one leaf at each clamshell side corner and one leaf at the top of the clamshell as shown, using the crease in the background to perfectly center the top leaf.

Begin adding leaves.

Pin Point Tip

WALK, DON'T RUN

My good quilting friend, Jennifer, and I began this appliqué project during the winter of 2020, when we were all confined to our homes during the initial outbreak of COVID. We seriously needed something fun to fill our days, and these appliqué pieces were just the thing.

I found that the key to really enjoying this project is to think of it as a walk, not a race. To do this, I set up a little workstation on my family-room coffee table which let me enjoy the company of my husband and doggos while prepping appliqués and treating myself to some guilty-pleasure TV. This approach let me stitch any time I had a few free minutes. I used large glass jars and filled them with my handiwork, which provided a bit of eye candy as I watched my piles grow, and they encouraged me to keep moving toward the finish line.

When tackling this project, remember that the turtle often wins the race!

Designed, appliquéd, and pieced by Kim Diehl. Machine quilted by Leisha Farnsworth.

5. Baste five additional leaves to each side of the clamshell, spacing them evenly between the previously positioned leaves as shown, to complete the design.

Place 13 leaves.

6. Use your favorite method to appliqué the clamshell blossom design, or use my invisible machine-appliqué stitching and finishing steps beginning on page 100. To simplify the machine stitching and eliminate the need for a lot of starts and stops, follow the continuous stitching path I used, which is shown below.

Machine appliqué stitching path.

7. Repeat steps 3–6 to appliqué 42 Clamshell Blossom blocks measuring 10½" × 9½", including the seam allowances.

Double-Take Tip

SCRAPPINESS WITH A PLAN

The featured scrappy quilt is very cheerful and colorful, but it takes on a whole different feel when made in the classic red-and-green color scheme using a planned scrappy approach. By "planned scrappy," I mean that there are two loosely planned versions of the block— red clamshells with scrappy green leaves, and green clamshells with scrappy red leaves. To stitch this quilt in the alternate color scheme, substitute 21 assorted red and 21 assorted green chubby sixteenths for the 42 assorted prints originally called for, and use the quilt pictured, right, as a guide while appliquéing and assembling your new classic design!

PIECING THE QUILT TOP

Sew all pieces with right sides together using a ¼" seam allowance unless otherwise noted. Press the seam allowances as indicated by the arrows or as otherwise specified.

Referring to the assembly diagram, right, lay out the Clamshell Blossom blocks in seven horizontal rows of six blocks each. Join the blocks in each row. Press. Join the rows. Press. The pieced quilt top should measure 54½" × 70½".

COMPLETING THE QUILT

Lay out and baste the quilt top, batting, and backing. Quilt the layers. The featured quilt is machine quilted with a different pattern in each clamshell, ranging from double curved and straight crosshatches to double lines positioned at different angles. The top blossom edge of

Quilt assembly

Simple Double-Dipped Quilts

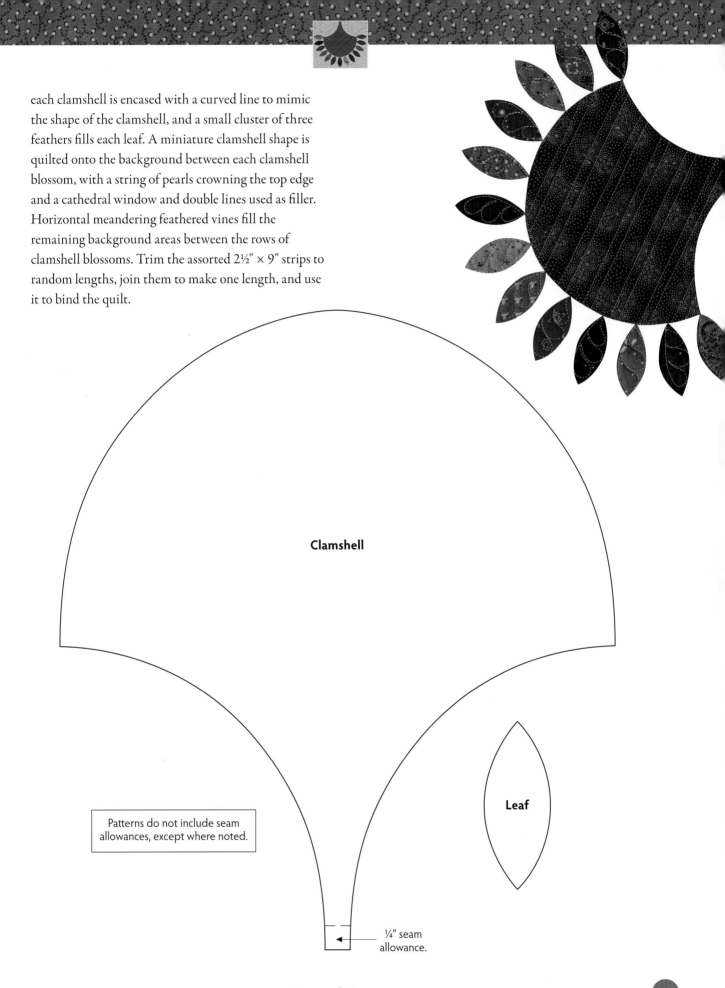

each clamshell is encased with a curved line to mimic the shape of the clamshell, and a small cluster of three feathers fills each leaf. A miniature clamshell shape is quilted onto the background between each clamshell blossom, with a string of pearls crowning the top edge and a cathedral window and double lines used as filler. Horizontal meandering feathered vines fill the remaining background areas between the rows of clamshell blossoms. Trim the assorted 2½" × 9" strips to random lengths, join them to make one length, and use it to bind the quilt.

Clamshell

Leaf

Patterns do not include seam allowances, except where noted.

¼" seam allowance.

Scrap Basket

Strippy Log Cabin blocks are charming and colorful, tried and true, and a go-to favorite for generations of quilters. So how could this block be double dipped for even more *charm and color? By mingling a handful of pieced logs among the whole logs! Logs made from patchwork squares add dimension, sparkle, and a touch of whimsy for a whole new take on tradition.*

FINISHED QUILT SIZE: 62½" × 62½" | **FINISHED BLOCK SIZE: 9" × 9"**

MATERIALS

Yardage is based on a 42" width of useable fabric after prewashing and removing selvages. See "Auditioning Prints" on page 26 for guidance on selecting fabrics for this quilt.

Approximately 80–100 fat sixteenths (4½" × 21½") in 13 groups of 6–8 dark prints for each color, or equivalent scraps, for Log Cabin A and B blocks and border

4 fat eighths (9" × 21") of assorted cream prints for Log Cabin A blocks

5 fat eighths of assorted cream prints for Log Cabin B blocks

⅔ yard of dark red print for Log Cabin A and B block center squares and binding

3⅞ yards of fabric for backing

69" × 69" square of quilt batting

Pin Point Tip

AUDITIONING PRINTS

I consider this quilt to be a planned scrappy design, meaning that many prints are used for the log cabin strips, with loosely planned placement of the colors that make up the coordinating pieced logs.

When selecting the prints for my quilt, I chose 13 basic colors: red, gold, light green, dark green, navy, orange, dark brown, medium brown, gray, teal, aqua, black, and pink. I used 6–8 assorted prints in each of these colors for the block patchwork. This may seem like a lot of fabrics, but the amounts needed are small. The number of colors you use is entirely up to you, but incorporating a total of 80–100 prints will give you lots of choices and versatility as you stitch the patchwork. Of course, if your stash allows, you can purchase a smaller number of prints than called for and supplement them with your on-hand scraps.

CUTTING

Scrap Basket is made of Log Cabin A and Log Cabin B blocks to create the design. For greater ease in piecing the blocks, cutting is listed below for the cream portions of the A and B blocks. Cutting for the assorted print portions of each block, as well as for the border, are provided separately in individual sections of the project directions. Cut all pieces across the width of the fabric in the order given unless otherwise noted.

From *each* of the 4 cream prints for the A blocks, cut:
5 strips, 1½" × 21"; crosscut into:
- 5 squares, 1½" × 1½" (combined total of 20)
- 5 rectangles, 1½" × 2½" (combined total of 20)
- 5 rectangles, 1½" × 5½" (combined total of 20)
- 5 rectangles, 1½" × 6½" (combined total of 20)

Label the above pieces as Log Cabin A cream patchwork set.

From *each* of the 5 cream prints for the B blocks, cut:
4 strips, 1½" × 21"; crosscut *each strip* into:
- 1 rectangle, 1½" × 3½" (combined total of 20)
- 1 rectangle, 1½" × 7½" (combined total of 20)
- 1 rectangle, 1½" × 8½" (combined total of 20)

1 strip, 1½" × 21"; crosscut into 4 rectangles, 1½" × 4½" (combined total of 20)

Label the above pieces as Log Cabin B cream patchwork set.

From the dark red print, cut:
2 strips, 1½" × 42"; crosscut into 36 squares, 1½" × 1½"
1 strip, 2½" × 42"; crosscut into 4 squares, 2½" × 2½". Add the remainder of the dark red 2½" strip to the strips that follow for binding.
6 binding strips, 2½" × 42" (For my chubby-binding method provided on page 103, reduce the strip width to 2".)

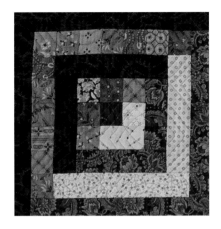

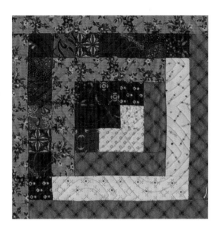

CUTTING FOR LOG CABIN A BLOCKS

From fat sixteenths of assorted prints, choose three different color groups that you feel will work well together in one block. For example, I chose navy, plum, and aqua for one block. Be adventurous with your choices and try combinations you might not usually pair together. It's fun to be surprised at the outcome!

From *all* of the prints included in the first color group (referred to as color A-1), cut a *combined total* of:

18 squares, 1½" × 1½", for the pieced logs in the top-left block corner

Reserve the remainder of the prints for use in the other blocks.

From *1* print in the second color group (referred to as color A-2), cut:

1 rectangle, 1½" × 3½"
1 rectangle, 1½" × 4½"
1 rectangle, 1½" × 7½"
1 rectangle, 1½" × 8½"

These pieces are for the outer whole logs in the bottom-right block corner. Reserve the remainder of the print for use in the other blocks.

From *1* print in the third color group (referred to as color A-3), cut:

1 rectangle, 1½" × 4½"
1 rectangle, 1½" × 5½"
1 rectangle, 1½" × 8½"
1 rectangle, 1½" × 9½"

These pieces are for the whole logs in the block corner that includes pieced logs. Reserve the remainder of the print for use in the other blocks.

PIECING THE LOG CABIN A BLOCKS

Sew all pieces with right sides together using a ¼" seam allowance unless otherwise noted. Press the seam allowances as indicated by the arrows or otherwise specified.

1. In addition to the dark print pieces listed in "Cutting for Log Cabin A Blocks," left, you also need one dark red 1½" square and the following assorted cream pieces from the Log Cabin A cream patchwork set for each block:

- 1 square, 1½" × 1½"
- 1 rectangle, 1½" × 2½"
- 1 rectangle, 1½" × 5½"
- 1 rectangle, 1½" × 6½"

Note: For my quilt, I divvied up the cream squares and rectangles so that each print would be used approximately once per block for good balance and variety.

2. Using the 1½" A-1 squares, join two squares to make a two-square log and three squares to make a three-square log, as shown. Press. In the same manner, piece a six-square log and a seven-square log. Press.

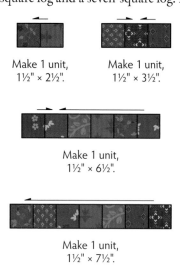

Make 1 unit,
1½" × 2½".

Make 1 unit,
1½" × 3½".

Make 1 unit,
1½" × 6½".

Make 1 unit,
1½" × 7½".

3. Join the red and cream 1½" squares. Press. Join the cream 1½" × 2½" rectangle to the bottom edge of the red and cream squares to make a unit that is 2½" square, including the seam allowances.

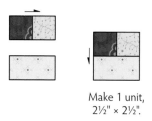

Make 1 unit,
2½" × 2½".

4. Join the A-1 two-square log to the top of the step 3 unit. Press. Join the A-1 three-square log to the left edge of the unit. Press. The Log Cabin A center unit should measure 3½" square, including the seam allowances.

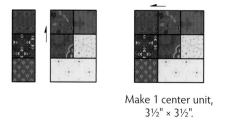

Make 1 center unit,
3½" × 3½".

5. Beginning at the right edge of the center unit, work in a clockwise direction to add the A-2 logs, the A-3 logs, and the remaining cream logs and A-1 pieced logs to complete the block rows as shown. Press all seam allowances away from the center unit.

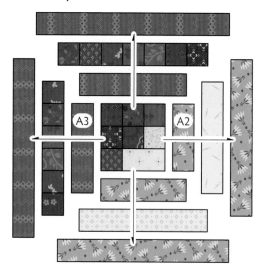

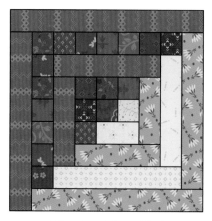

Make 1 Log Cabin A block,
9½" × 9½".

6. Repeat steps 1–5 using the remaining cream pieces, the assorted prints, and scraps (as scraps allow) to piece a total of 18 Log Cabin A blocks measuring 9½" square, including the seam allowances. You'll have a small handful of unused cream pieces from the Log Cabin A cream patchwork set; these have been included for added choices as you piece the blocks.

CUTTING FOR LOG CABIN B BLOCKS

From all of the assorted prints, including the remainder of any scraps from making the A blocks, choose three different color groups that you feel will work together in one block.

From *all* of the prints in the first color group (referred to as color B-1), cut a *combined total* of:

14 squares, 1½" × 1½", for the pieced logs in the light block corner

Reserve the remainder of the prints for use in the other blocks.

From *all* of the prints in the second color group (referred to as color B-2), cut a *combined total* of:

18 squares, 1½" × 1½", for the pieced logs in the diagonally opposite dark block corner containing the first set of pieced logs

Reserve the remainder of the prints for use in the other blocks.

From *1* print in the third color group (referred to as color B-3), cut:

1 rectangle, 1½" × 4½"

1 rectangle, 1½" × 5½"

1 rectangle, 1½" × 8½"

1 rectangle, 1½" × 9½"

These pieces are for the whole logs in the dark block corner diagonally opposite the cream logs.

Reserve the remainder of the print for use in the other blocks.

PIECING THE LOG CABIN B BLOCKS

1. In addition to the dark print pieces listed in "Cutting for Log Cabin B Blocks," left, you also need one dark red 1½" square and the following pieces of assorted cream prints from the Log Cabin B cream patchwork set for each block:

- 1 rectangle, 1½" × 3½"
- 1 rectangle, 1½" × 4½"
- 1 rectangle, 1½" × 7½"
- 1 rectangle, 1½" × 8½"

Note: As for the Log Cabin A blocks, I chose cream rectangles so that each print would be used approximately once per block for good balance and variety.

2. Using the 1½" B-1 squares, join two squares to make a two-square log and five squares to make a five-square log. Press both units. In the same manner, make a six-square log. Press. Reserve the pieced B-1 logs and the remaining 1½" B-1 square for later steps.

Make 1 unit, 1½" × 2½".   Make 1 unit, 1½" × 5½".

Make 1 unit, 1½" × 6½".

3. Repeat step 2 using all 18 of the 1½" B-2 squares to piece a two-square log, a three-square log, a six-square log, and a seven-square log.

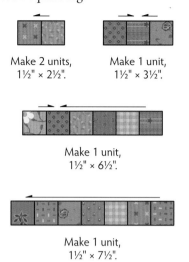

Make 2 units,
1½" × 2½".

Make 1 unit,
1½" × 3½".

Make 1 unit,
1½" × 6½".

Make 1 unit,
1½" × 7½".

4. Join the reserved B-1 and the dark red 1½" squares. Press. Join the two-square B-2 log to the right edge of the unit as shown. Press. The pieced unit should measure 2½" square, including the seam allowances.

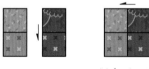

Make 1 unit,
2½" × 2½".

5. Join the two-square B-1 log to the right of the unit from step 4 as shown. Press. Join the three-square B-2 log to the top edge of the unit. Press. The pieced Log Cabin B center unit should measure 3½" square, including the seam allowances.

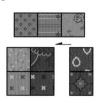

Make 1 center unit,
3½" × 3½".

6. Referring to the illustration and beginning at the right edge of the center unit, work in a clockwise direction to add the cream logs, the remaining B-1 and B-2 pieced logs, and the B-3 whole logs to form the block rows. Press.

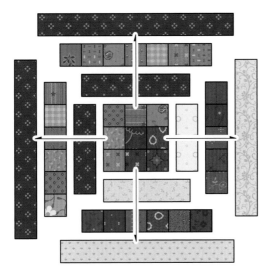

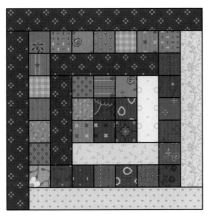

Make 1 Log Cabin B block,
9½" × 9½".

7. Repeat steps 1–6 using the remaining assorted prints, as well as scraps, to piece a total of 18 Log Cabin B blocks measuring 9½" square, including the seam allowances. You'll have a small handful of unused cream rectangles from the Log Cabin B cream patchwork set; these have been included for added choices as you piece the blocks. Reserve all assorted print scraps for use in the border.

Pin Point Tip

STEP UP YOUR PACE!

Piecing the Log Cabin blocks one at a time is a good, methodical way to accomplish the patchwork, but it's easy to multitask and tackle them three or four at a time as I did. After completing the cutting and steps 1–4 for three or four blocks at a time, lay out the pieced center unit and coordinating logs chosen for one block onto a large square acrylic ruler or a felt block design board. (Having one completed block on hand to refer to as you lay out the pieces is helpful.) Continue laying out the blocks one at a time, layering new pieces onto the previously laid out block. Transport the ruler between your sewing machine and ironing board, piecing and pressing the block rows one by one. Use the components that remain on the ruler to help reposition the in-progress patchwork, and you'll step up your speed!

Designed and pieced by Kim Diehl. Machine quilted by Connie Tabor.

Simple Double-Dipped Quilts

PIECING THE QUILT CENTER

1. Lay out two Log Cabin A and two Log Cabin B blocks with like blocks in diagonally opposite corners from one another as shown. Join the blocks in each row. Press. Join the rows. Press. Repeat to piece a total of nine four-block units measuring 18½" square, including the seam allowances.

2. Lay out nine four-block units in three rows of three units each, rotating the center unit in each row 180° so the horizontal seams will nest together. Join the units in rows. Press. Join the top, center, and bottom rows. Press. The pieced quilt center should measure 54½" square.

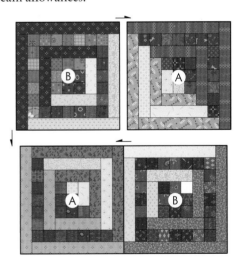

Make nine 4-block units, 18½" × 18½".

Quilt assembly

CUTTING FOR THE BORDER

From the scraps that remain from all assorted prints, cut a *combined total* of:

180 rectangles, 1½" × 4½"

8 rectangles, 1½" × 3½"

4 rectangles, 1½" × 2½"

160 squares, 1½" × 1½", in sets of 4 (each set should be 4 different prints from the same color family; group the sets together by color family)

PIECING AND ADDING THE BORDER

1. Join each set of four squares cut from a single color to make a total of 40 pieced logs measuring 1½" × 4½", including the seam allowances.

Make 40 units,
1½" × 4½".

2. Choosing the prints randomly and referring to the diagram, lay out 44 assorted print 1½" × 4½" whole logs and 10 pieced logs side by side. (You can follow the layout in the illustration to space your pieced rectangles among the whole rectangles or create your own layout.) Join the pieces to create a border strip measuring 4½" × 54½", including the seam allowances. Press. Repeat to piece a total of four border strips.

Note: For the sake of easier, speedier pressing, I pressed the seam allowances in each border strip all in one direction. When I joined the border strips to the quilt center, if there was an occasional seam that would be better pressed in the opposite direction to nest with the seam it would be resting against, I took a quick moment to re-press the seam in the opposite direction.

Make 4 border strips,
4½" × 54½".

3. Join patchwork border strips to the right and left side of the quilt center. Press the seam allowances toward the quilt center.

4. Lay out a dark red 2½" square, one print 1½" × 2½" rectangle, two print 1½" × 3½" rectangles, and one print 1½" × 4½" rectangle as shown. Working outward from the red square, join the pieces to build a corner patchwork unit. Press. Repeat to piece a total of four corner units measuring 4½" square, including the seam allowances.

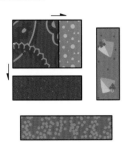
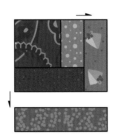

Make 4 corner units,
4½" × 4½".

5. Referring to the quilt pictured on page 32, join a corner patchwork unit to each end of the remaining patchwork border strips from step 2, with the dark red squares on the top outer corners. Press the seam allowances toward the corner units. Join these completed border strips to the top and bottom of the quilt center, with the dark red squares in the outer corners. Press the seam allowances toward the quilt center. The completed quilt top should measure 62½" square.

COMPLETING THE QUILT

Layer and baste the quilt top, batting, and backing. Quilt the layers. The featured quilt is machine quilted with an edge-to-edge horizontal design of plump almond shapes that echo outward to form a ripple effect, with placement of the almond shapes in every other row staggered to fill the top seamlessly. Join the dark red binding strips to make one length and use it to bind the quilt.

Double-Take Tip

WHEN THE STARS ALIGN

Adjusting the positions of the cream prints in two strategically placed Log Cabin A and two Log Cabin B blocks creates a subtle star shape in the center, instead of the repeating diamond shapes in the featured quilt.

For this option, substitute four 1½"-wide cream logs in 4½", 5½", 8½", and 9½" lengths for the whole logs in the outer corner of two A blocks (these will become the corner blocks between the upper-left and bottom-right blocks that form the star points). Next, substitute four 1½"-wide cream logs in 4½", 5½", 8½", and 9½" lengths for the whole logs in the outer corner of two B blocks (these will become the corner blocks between the upper-right and bottom-left blocks that form the star points). I've outlined the star in pink so you can easily see the transformation. If you're head over heels for star quilts, you'll love the result!

Alternate layout

Slapdash

One of my very favorite blocks is the traditional Churn Dash, so of course I had to double dip it! With a goal of enhancing rather than substantially changing this time-honored block, I focused on a creative approach to coloring it; I replaced strategic portions of the cream background with light and dark shades of gray, bringing the illusion of layers and ramping up the wow factor.

FINISHED QUILT SIZE: 84½" × 84½" | **FINISHED BLOCK SIZE: 12" × 12"**

MATERIALS

Yardage is based on a 42" width of useable fabric after prewashing and removing selvages.

13 fat quarters (18" × 21") of assorted prints for the Churn Dash portion of the blocks

7 yards of light gray print for the shaded background portion of the blocks

2⅝ yards of dark gray print for the block center squares and binding

2½ yards of cream print for the background portions of the blocks

2½ yards of 108"-wide fabric *OR* 7⅝ yards of 42"-wide fabric for backing

91" × 91" square of batting

CUTTING

Cut all pieces across the width of the fabric in the order given unless otherwise noted.

From *each* of the 13 assorted prints, cut:

3 strips, 2¾" × 21"; crosscut into 16 squares, 2¾" × 2¾"

4 strips, 1½" × 21" (If you don't prewash your fabrics, you can likely reduce the number of strips to 3 and still cut the needed units.)

Keep the pieces organized by print into 13 Churn Dash patchwork sets; each set will yield 4 identical blocks.

From the light gray print, cut:

26 strips, 5" × 42"; crosscut into 208 squares, 5" × 5"

26 strips, 4" × 42"; cut each strip in half crosswise to yield 2 strips, 4" × 21", for a combined total of 52. (If you don't prewash your fabrics, you can likely reduce the number of strips to 20, and then crosscut them to yield a total of 40 strips, 21" long, and still cut the needed units.)

From the dark gray print, cut:

15 strips, 2¾" × 42"; crosscut into 208 squares, 2¾" × 2¾"

5 strips, 3½" × 42"; crosscut into 52 squares, 3½" × 3½"

9 binding strips, 2½" × 42" (For my chubby-binding method provided on page 103, reduce the strip width to 2".)

From the cream print, cut:

29 strips, 2¾" × 42"; crosscut into 416 squares, 2¾" × 2¾"

PIECING THE CHURN DASH BLOCKS

Sew all pieces with right sides together using a ¼" seam allowance unless otherwise specified. Press the seam allowances as indicated by the arrows or as otherwise specified.

1. The blocks are made in sets of four identical blocks. For each set of four blocks you will need:

- 1 matching-print Churn Dash patchwork set
- 16 light gray 5" squares (4 per block)
- 4 light gray 4" × 21" strips
- 16 dark gray 2¾" squares (4 per block)
- 4 dark gray 3½" squares (1 per block)
- 32 cream 2¾" squares (8 per block)

2. Use a pencil and an acrylic ruler to draw a diagonal sewing line from corner to corner on the wrong side of each cream and dark gray 2¾" square. Repeat to prepare the Churn Dash print 2¾" squares.

3. Layer prepared cream 2¾" squares onto two opposite corners of a light gray 5" square. Stitch the squares along the drawn diagonal lines. Fold the resulting inner triangles open, aligning the corners with the corner of the light gray square. Press. Trim away the layers beneath the top triangles, leaving a ¼" seam allowance. Repeat to piece a total of 16 units, 5" square, including the seam allowances.

Make 16 pieced squares,
5" × 5".

4. Repeat step 3 using the prepared dark gray and Churn Dash matching-print 2¾" squares and the units from step 3 to piece 16 corner units measuring 5" square.

Make 16 corner units,
5" × 5".

5. Join a light gray 4" × 21" strip and a Churn Dash print 1½" × 21" strip along the long edges to make a strip set. Press. Repeat to piece four strip sets, 5" × 21", including the seam allowances. Cut the strip sets at 3½" intervals to yield a total of 16 units, 5" × 3½", including the seam allowances.

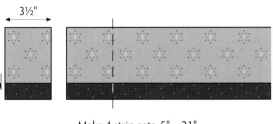

Make 4 strip sets, 5" × 21".
Cut 16 segments, 5" × 3½".

6. Lay out four units from step 5, four corner units from step 4, and one dark gray 3½" square in three horizontal rows as shown. Join the pieces in each row. Press. Join the rows. Press. Repeat to piece four identical Churn Dash blocks measuring 12½" square, including the seam allowances.

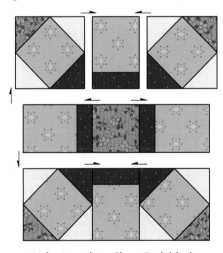

Make 4 matching Churn Dash blocks,
12½" × 12½".

7. Using the remaining Churn Dash patchwork sets, repeat steps 1–6 to piece four identical blocks from *each* Churn Dash print for a combined total of 52 Churn Dash blocks.

slow.
deep.
quiet.
in everything
you do.

(in case you forgot
again because of
all that other stuff
on your list...)

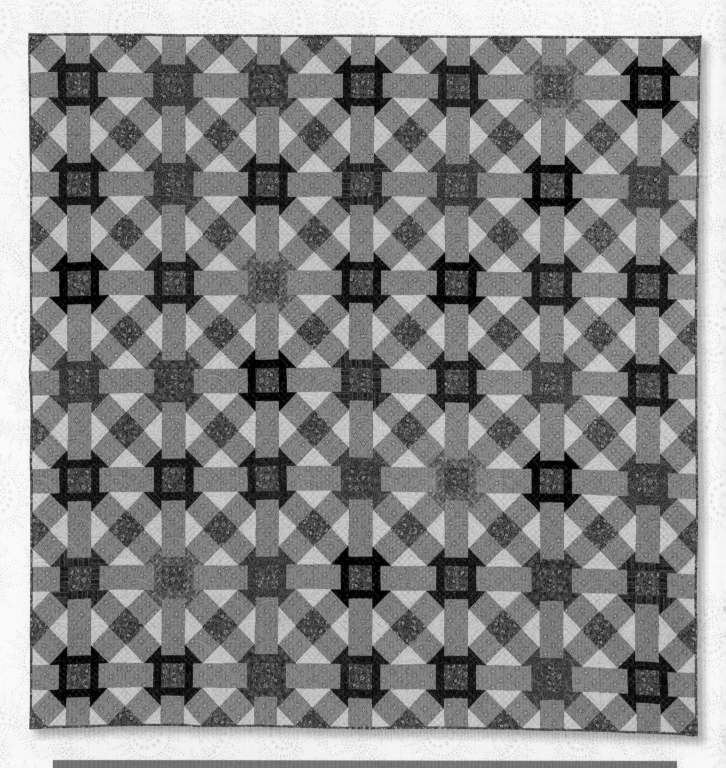

Designed by Kim Diehl. Pieced by Jennifer Martinez and Kim Diehl. Machine quilted by Connie Tabor.

Simple Double-Dipped Quilts

PIECING THE QUILT TOP

1. Lay out the Churn Dash blocks in seven horizontal rows of seven blocks each. Please note that you'll have three unused blocks; these have been included for added versatility as you lay out the quilt center. See "Rescue Your Orphan Blocks," right, for tips on using these extras.

2. Join the blocks in each horizontal row. Press. Join the rows. Press. The pieced quilt top should measure 84½" square.

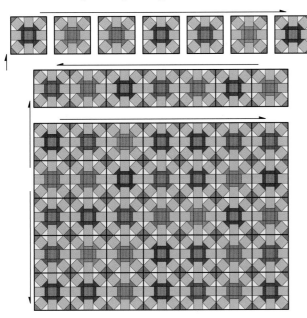

Quilt assembly

COMPLETING THE QUILT

Layer and baste the quilt top, batting, and backing. Quilt the layers. The featured quilt is machine quilted with an edge-to-edge crosshatched clamshell design. Join the dark gray binding strips together to make one length and use it to bind the quilt.

Pin Point Tip

RESCUE YOUR ORPHAN BLOCKS

Instead of letting your leftover Churn Dash blocks become "orphans" that languish in a drawer, consider using them to give yourself an unexpected gift. Here are three quick and easy ideas to try:

- Use each block individually as is or add simple borders to make throw pillows in any size you choose.

- Join the three leftover blocks end to end for a 12½" × 36½" quilted table runner that can be finished in a jiffy.

- Join the three blocks end to end as noted above, layer the pieced unit with batting and backing, quilt the layers, and then finish with a pillow backing and Polyfil stuffing to whip up a sweet lumbar pillow to complement your bed quilt.

Double-Take Tip

A SWITCH THAT'S EASY AS 1-2-3

To easily change the look of this quilt and provide an expanded canvas for some beautiful hand or machine quilting, you can swap the color of the vertical and horizontal strip-set background pieces that form the shaded portion of the blocks from light gray to cream. If you decide to give this alternate version a try, simply reduce the amount of the light gray print by 3 yards and increase the cream print by the same amount. One simple quilt pattern, two distinctly different choices for the finished look of your quilt!

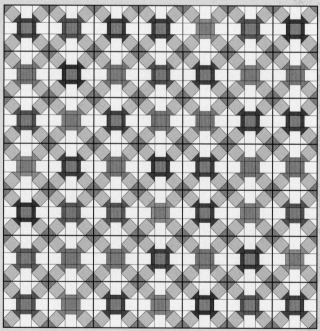

Alternate layout

Dillydallying

When creating this sweet mini design I decided to double down and use the humble
Nine Patch block in two ways. One block style uses strategically placed medium- and dark-hued
squares to create the illusion of layers, while the second block is fashioned entirely from
light shirting prints to form a charming creamy checkerboard, letting the "flashy" blocks be the stars.

FINISHED QUILT SIZE: 9½" × 13½" | **FINISHED BLOCK SIZE: 3" × 3"**

MATERIALS

Yardage is based on a 42" width of useable fabric after
prewashing and removing selvages.

5 charm squares (5" × 5") of assorted prints for
Plus Sign blocks

5 squares, 1½" × 1½", of assorted prints for Plus Sign
block centers, each in a deeper shade of the 5 prints
called for above

Assorted small-scale cream print scraps, enough to cut
56 squares, 1½" × 1½", for Plus Sign block corners and
Cream Checkerboard blocks

36 squares, 1½" × 1½", of assorted print scraps for
patchwork border

1 fat quarter (18" × 21") of black print for patchwork
border and binding

1 fat quarter of fabric for backing

14" × 18" rectangle of batting

CUTTING

Cut all pieces across the width of the fabric in the order given unless otherwise noted.

From *each* of the 5 assorted print charm squares, cut:
4 squares, 1½" × 1½" (combined total of 20)
Keep the squares organized by print, along with
    one coordinating 1½" darker square, into 5 plus-sign
    patchwork sets.

From the scraps of assorted cream prints, cut a *combined total* of:
56 squares, 1½" × 1½"

From the scraps of assorted prints, cut a *combined total* of:
36 squares, 1½" × 1½"
Keep these assorted print 1½" squares organized into
    a border patchwork set.

From the black print, cut:
1 strip, 2½" × 21"; crosscut into 8 squares, 2½" × 2½"
3 binding strips, 2½" × 21". (For my chubby-binding
    method provided on page 103, reduce the strip
    width to 2".)

PIECING THE PLUS SIGN BLOCKS

Sew all pieces with right sides together using a ¼" seam allowance unless otherwise noted. Press the seam allowances as indicated by the arrows or as otherwise specified.

Select a plus-sign patchwork set and four assorted cream print 1½" squares. Lay out the squares in three horizontal rows as shown. Join the squares in each row. Press. Join the rows. Press. Repeat to piece a total of five Plus Sign blocks measuring 3½" square, including the seam allowances.

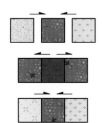

Make 5 blocks,
3½" × 3½".

Pin Point Tip

CREATING A GO-TO STASH OF LITTLE SQUARES

Before cleaning up or tossing my leftover scraps when cutting fabrics for a quilt project, I take a few moments to cut a handful of 1½" squares from the leftovers to use in future scrappy projects. These squares can be dropped into a glass canister or a hurricane jar for practical *and* pretty storage, and my little stash of squares comes in handy for stitching checkerboards, colorful star points, and so much more. For this Dillydallying project, I was able to raid my stash jar, chose my precut squares, and take advantage of a nice little shortcut to save a bit of time. Give this stashed-squares approach a try, and I'm guessing that you'll find it comes in handy, too!

PIECING THE CREAM CHECKERBOARD BLOCKS

Select nine assorted cream print 1½" squares. Lay out the squares in three horizontal rows. Join the squares in each row. Press. Join the rows. Press. Repeat to piece a total of four Cream Checkerboard blocks measuring 3½" square, including the seam allowances.

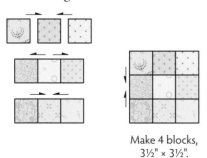

Make 4 blocks,
3½" × 3½".

PIECING THE QUILT CENTER

Lay out the five Plus Sign blocks and the four Cream Checkerboard blocks in three horizontal rows as shown, orienting the Cream Checkerboard blocks so the pressed seams will nest together with those of the Plus Sign blocks. Join the blocks in each row. Press. Join the rows. Press. The pieced quilt center should measure 9½" square, including the seam allowances.

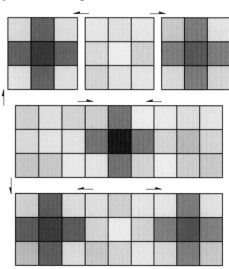

Make 1 quilt center,
9½" × 9½".

Simple Double-Dipped Quilts

Designed, pieced, and hand quilted by Kim Diehl.

2. Use a pencil and an acrylic ruler to draw a diagonal sewing line from corner to corner on the wrong side of each black 2½" square. Layer a prepared square onto a four-patch unit. Stitch the pair together along the drawn diagonal line. Press one of the resulting black triangles open to expose your favorite half of the four-patch unit, aligning the black corner with the corner of the four patch beneath. Press. Trim away the layers beneath the top black triangle, leaving a ¼" seam allowance. Repeat to piece a total of eight checkerboard-triangle squares measuring 2½" square, including the seam allowances.

Make 8 units,
2½" × 2½".

3. Join the four reserved assorted print 1½" squares to make two two-patch units measuring 1½" × 2½", including the seam allowances. Press.

Make 2 units,
1½" × 2½".

PIECING AND ADDING THE BORDER

1. Select the border patchwork set. Choosing the prints randomly, lay out four assorted print 1½" squares in two horizontal rows. Join the squares in each row. Press. Join the rows. Press. Repeat to piece a total of eight four-patch units measuring 2½" square, including the seam allowances. Reserve the remaining four assorted print 1½" squares for later use.

4. Lay out four checkerboard-triangle squares from step 2 and one two-patch unit as shown. Join the pieces. Press. Repeat to piece two border strips measuring 2½" × 9½", including the seam allowances.

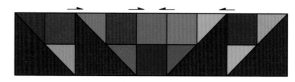

Make 2 borders,
2½" × 9½".

Make 8 units,
2½" × 2½".

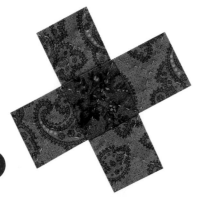

5. Referring to the diagram below, join the two pieced border strips to the quilt center, orienting them as shown. Press.

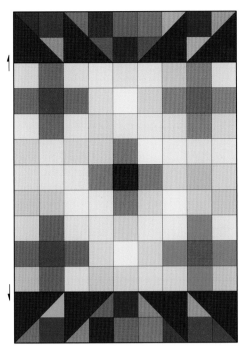

Adding borders

COMPLETING THE QUILT

Layer and baste the quilt top, batting, and backing. Quilt the layers. The featured quilt is hand quilted with a diagonal crosshatch design over the blocks in the quilt center. The quilted crosshatch design is repeated on the border checkerboard squares, with repeating straight diagonal lines stitched onto the black triangles. Join the black binding strips together to make one length and use it to bind the quilt.

Double-Take Tip

A CONVENTIONAL SHIFT FOR THE WIN!

Instead of using the Cream Checkerboard blocks as in the featured quilt, think about substituting more conventional Nine Patch blocks that are colored in the traditional way using light and dark prints. Pairing the plus-sign patchwork with traditional Nine Patch blocks has the effect of adding more color and creates a subtly unique twist on the classic checkerboard that we all love so much.

Alternate layout

Dillydallying

Raising the Roof

Because I use half-square triangles in so many of my quilts, I wondered . . . could such a basic block be double dipped to add a twist? Challenge accepted! With the addition of stitch-and-fold corner triangles and a diagonal center strip, the scrappy Fractured Half-Square-Triangle block was born. Big, chunky pieces, and no block seams to match, make this design a dream to stitch.

FINISHED QUILT SIZE: 60½" × 60½" | **FINISHED BLOCK SIZE: 6" × 6"**

MATERIALS

Yardage is based on a 42" width of useable fabric after prewashing and removing selvages.

35 fat eighths (9" × 21") of assorted medium and dark prints (referred to as "dark") for blocks

7 fat quarters (18" × 21") of assorted cream prints for blocks

Approximately ½ yard of assorted print scraps for block center strips

⅝ yard of complementary print for binding

3¾ yards of fabric for backing

67" × 67" square of batting

Piecing the Fractured Half-Square-Triangle Block

Sew all pieces with right sides together using a ¼" seam allowance unless otherwise noted. Press the seam allowances as indicated by the arrows or otherwise specified.

1. Use a pencil and an acrylic ruler to draw a diagonal sewing line from corner to corner on the wrong side of each cream 3" square.

2. Choosing the cream prints randomly, layer and stitch prepared cream 3" squares to two opposite corners of a 6¼" dark print square as shown. Fold the resulting inner triangles open, aligning the corners with the corners of the large bottom square. Press. Trim away the layers beneath the top triangles, leaving ¼" seam allowances. Repeat to piece a total of 105 units measuring 6¼" square, including the seam allowances.

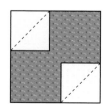 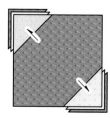

Make 105 units, 6¼" × 6¼".

Cutting

Cut all pieces across the width of the fabric in the order given unless otherwise noted.

From *each* of the 35 assorted dark prints, cut:

1 strip, 6¼" × 21"; crosscut into 3 squares, 6¼" × 6¼" (combined total of 105)

1 strip, 1½" × 21"; crosscut into 2 strips, 1½" × 10" (combined total of 70)

From *each* of the 7 assorted cream prints, cut:

5 strips, 3" × 21"; crosscut into 30 squares, 3" × 3" (combined total of 210)

From the assorted print scraps, cut:

35 strips, 1½" × 10" (combined total of 105 with previously cut strips)

From the print for binding, cut:

7 strips, 2½" × 42" (For my chubby-binding method provided on page 103, reduce the strip width to 2".)

3. Use a rotary cutter and an acrylic ruler to cut each pieced unit from step 2 in half diagonally as shown. Fold each resulting triangle in half to find the center and gently finger-press the crease at the long diagonal edge.

Cut.

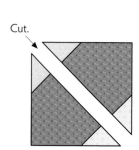 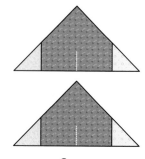

Crease.

4. Choose a prepared triangle unit from step 3 and a complementary 1½" × 10" dark print strip. Have fun with your color choices and try combinations you might not ordinarily use; you can't make a mistake! Fold the strip in half crosswise to find the center and finger-press the crease. Align the creases of the strip and the triangle to perfectly center them from right to left and pin in place. Stitch the strip to the triangle. Press. Repeat to piece a total of 210 half-block units.

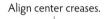

Align center creases.

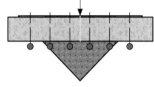

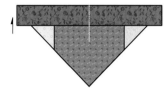

5. Choose a half-block unit from step 4 and a prepared triangle unit from step 3. Align and join the units as instructed in step 4. Press. Repeat to piece a total of 105 Fractured Half-Square-Triangle blocks measuring 6½" square, including the seam allowances.

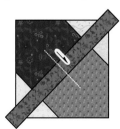

Make 105 blocks,
6½" × 6½".

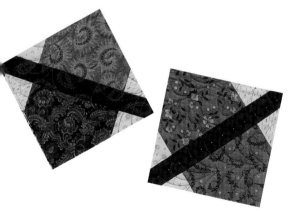

Pin Point Tip

TRIANGLE SHORTCUT

There are many methods and specialty notions available for piecing stitch-and-fold triangles as used in this quilt. To keep things simple, you'll find the traditional drawn-line technique provided in each of my books to enable you to sew the patchwork without requiring the purchase of additional tools. With that said, you can always substitute your own preferred technique. I enjoy stitching more than drawing lines, so here's my favorite shortcut to eliminate the line-drawing step:

First, rest an acrylic ruler against the left side of the machine needle, with the needle in the down position. Use a fine-tipped permanent black marker to draw a line along the ruler's edge from the feed-dog opening to the front of the sewing-machine bed. (If you'd rather not mark a line, painter's masking tape or quarter-inch quilter's tape works equally well.)

Next, for more visibility as you sew, snap the open-toe foot or a foot with an acrylic insert onto your sewing machine.

Last, position the patchwork with the corner of the top layered square aligned at the needle and the bottom corner point resting on the center of the drawn line. As you stitch, slide the bottom corner of the layered patchwork along the drawn line to perfectly center the seam. Complete the final steps as instructed in the project directions. You'll find this technique to be a great time-saver, and you'll love the accurate results!

Raising the Roof

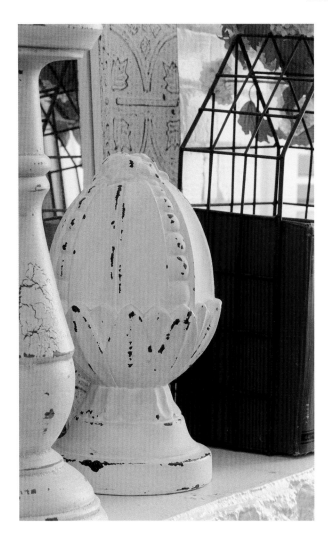

Piecing the Quilt Top

1. Referring to the illustration, lay out 25 blocks in five horizontal rows of five blocks each with the center strips running diagonally from bottom left to upper right. Join the blocks in each row. Press. Join the rows. Press. Repeat to piece two quilt-center quadrants measuring 30½" square, including the seam allowances.

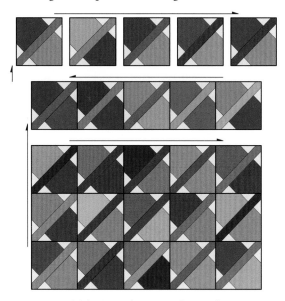

Make 2 quadrants, 30½" × 30½".

6. Use a rotary cutter and a square acrylic ruler with a center diagonal line to trim the excess strip length at the corners of the blocks, ensuring the ruler's diagonal line is centered over the pieced rectangle to square up the block and produce uniformly positioned seams. Please note that you'll have five unused blocks; these have been included for added choices and versatility as you lay out the quilt design.

2. In the same manner, piece two mirror-image quilt-center quadrants with the center strips running from top left to bottom right as shown.

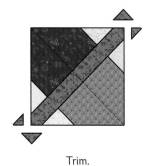

Trim.

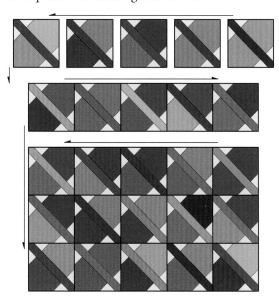

Make 2 quadrants, 30½" × 30½".

Simple Double-Dipped Quilts

Designed and pieced by Kim Diehl. Machine quilted by Connie Tabor.

Raising the Roof

3. Using the assembly diagram, right, as a guide, lay out the four pieced quadrants in two horizontal rows, turning the quadrants as needed to achieve the pictured design. Join the quadrants in each row. Press. Join the rows. Press. The pieced quilt top should measure 60½" square.

COMPLETING THE QUILT

Layer and baste the quilt top, batting, and backing. Quilt the layers. The featured quilt is machine quilted with repeated rows of edge-to-edge serpentine feathered vines running horizontally across the quilt top. Join the complementary print binding strips together to make one length and use it to bind the quilt.

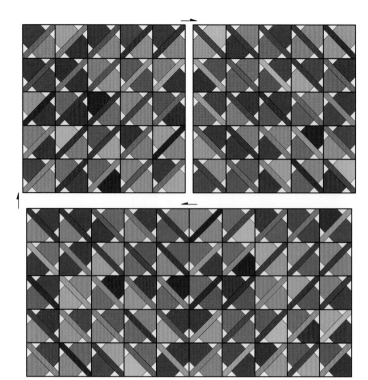

Quilt assembly

Double-Take Tip

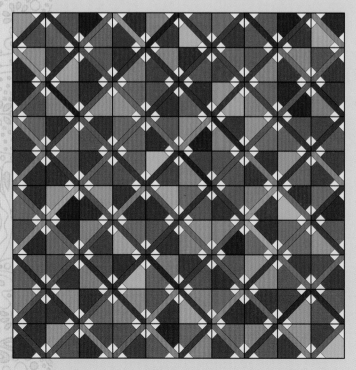

Alternate layout

ARGYLE, ANYONE?

The simply pieced Fractured Half-Square-Triangle block created for this book brings a myriad of setting options to the table for uniquely different looks. Here's an alternate setting idea inspired by argyle socks to spark your creativity. With an open mind and an adventurous spirit, you can discover and create even more gorgeous settings!

Huckle Buckle

What happens when you begin with a traditional pinwheel, add a frame of patchwork, and then extend the pinwheel paddles into the outer block corners? A little bit of magic! This double-dipped Pinwheel block looks rich and scrappy, gives your quilt a fantastic sense of movement, and is a total snap to piece.

FINISHED QUILT SIZE: 19½" × 19½" | **FINISHED BLOCK SIZE: 4" × 4"**

MATERIALS

Yardage is based on a 42" width of useable fabric after prewashing and removing selvages.

15 bitty bricks (4½" × 10½") of assorted prints for blocks

Scraps of assorted prints for sashing

1 fat quarter (18" × 21") of dark print for blocks and binding

1 fat eighth (9" × 21") of cream print #1 for pinwheels

1 fat quarter of cream print #2 for blocks and sashing

⅔ yard of fabric for backing

24" × 24" square of batting

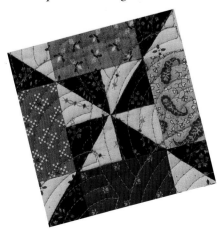

CUTTING

Cut all pieces across the width of the fabric in the order given unless otherwise noted.

From *each* of the 15 bitty bricks of assorted prints, cut:

1 strip, 2" × 10½"; crosscut into 4 squares, 2" × 2"
(combined total of 60; organize the squares in
groups of 4 matching-print squares to make
15 pinwheel sets)

1 strip, 1½" × 10½"; crosscut into:

- 1 rectangle, 1½" × 2½" (combined total of
  15 for block frames)
- 1 square, 1½" × 1½" (combined total of
  15 for sashing)

From the dark print, cut:

5 binding strips, 2½" × 21" (For my chubby-binding
method provided on page 103, reduce the strip
width to 2".)

1 strip, 2" × 21"; crosscut into 4 squares, 2" × 2". From
the remainder of the strip, cut 1 rectangle,
1½" × 2½", and 1 square, 1½" × 1½". (Keep the 2"
squares together in a pinwheel set for a combined
total of 16 sets with the previously cut sets. Add the
rectangles to the block-frame set and the squares to
the sashing set.)

From cream print #1, cut:

4 strips, 2" × 21"; crosscut into 32 squares, 2" × 2"

From cream print #2, cut:

4 strips, 2" × 21"; crosscut into 32 squares, 2" × 2"
4 strips, 1½" × 21"; crosscut into:

- 24 rectangles, 1½" × 2½"
- 9 squares, 1½" × 1½"

From the assorted print scraps, cut a *combined* *total* of:

48 rectangles, 1½" × 2½"

32 squares, 1½" × 1½" (For added choices as you piece
the patchwork, you may wish to cut an extra
handful of pieces in each given size.)

Add the rectangles to the block-frame set and the
squares to the sashing set.

PIECING THE FRAMED PINWHEEL BLOCKS

*Sew all pieces with right sides together using a ¼"
seam allowance unless otherwise noted. Press the seam
allowances as indicated by the arrows or otherwise
specified.*

My friend Jennifer and I shared the patchwork for
this mini quilt, and since we each have our own favorite
method of sewing half-square-triangle units, I decided
to share both and let you choose the approach you prefer.
If one or both of these techniques is new to you, consider
trying each of them—you may discover a new favorite!

1. Choose a pinwheel patchwork set, two *each* of the
2" cream #1 and cream #2 squares, and four assorted
print 1½" × 2½" rectangles from the block-frame set.
Two methods for stitching the pinwheel print and the
cream 2" squares to form half-square-triangle units are
outlined below; choose your preferred method or
substitute your own favorite technique.

Method 1. Use a pencil and an acrylic ruler to
draw a diagonal line from corner to corner on the
wrong side of each of the four cream 2" squares. Layer
each prepared cream square onto a 2" pinwheel print
square, right sides together. Snap a ¼" foot onto your
sewing machine and sew the pairs together ¼" from
each side of the drawn diagonal lines. Cut each stitched
pair apart along the drawn center line to yield a
combined total of eight pieced triangles, four from
cream #1 and four from cream #2.

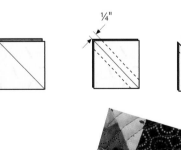

Method 2. Use a pencil and an acrylic ruler to draw *two* diagonal sewing lines onto each of the four cream 2" squares, ¼" away from each side of the corner point. (A tool such as the Fons & Porter Quarter Inch Seam Marker is great for this method.) Layer each prepared cream square onto a 2" pinwheel print square, right sides together. Snap an open-toe foot onto your sewing machine to easily see the drawn lines as you stitch. Sew the pairs together along both drawn lines. Cut the stitched pairs apart from corner to corner between the stitched seams to yield a combined total of eight pieced triangles, four from cream #1 and four from cream #2.

2. Press each stitched triangle open to make a half-square-triangle unit. Use a rotary cutter and an acrylic ruler to trim each unit to 1½" square, removing the dog-ear points in the same step.

Make 4 units.   Make 4 units.

3. Lay out the four cream #1 half-square-triangle units in two horizontal rows of two units to form a pinwheel design. Join the units. Press. Join the rows. Press. The pieced center pinwheel unit should measure 2½" square, including the seam allowances.

Make 1 pinwheel unit,
2½" × 2½".

4. Lay out the pinwheel unit, four assorted print 1½" × 2½" rectangles, and the four cream #2 half-square-triangle units in three horizontal rows as shown. Join the pieces in each row. Press. Join the rows and press to complete a Framed Pinwheel block that measures 4½" square, including the seam allowances.

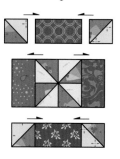
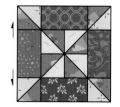

Make 1 Framed Pinwheel block,
4½" × 4½".

5. Repeat steps 1–4 to piece a total of 16 Framed Pinwheel blocks.

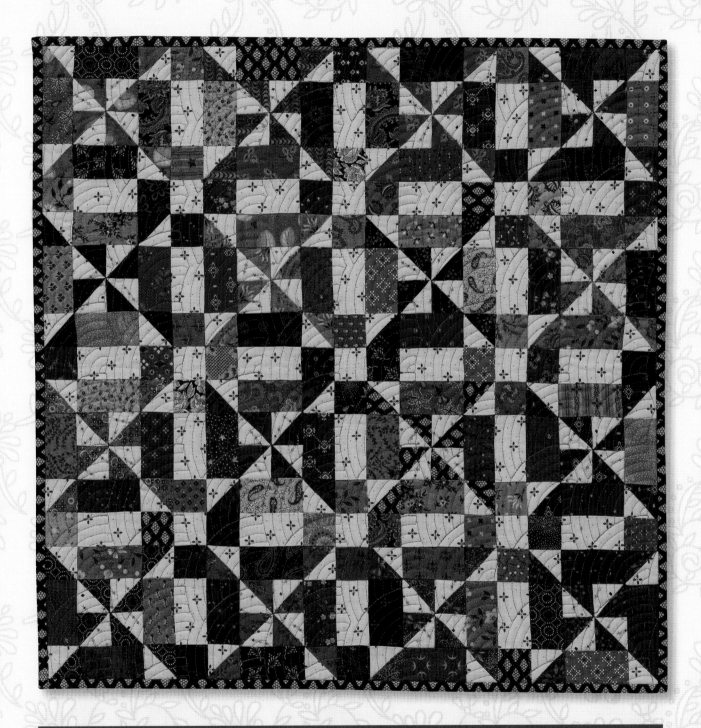

Designed by Kim Diehl. Pieced by Jennifer Martinez and Kim Diehl. Machine quilted by Connie Tabor.

PIECING THE SASHING STRIPS

1. Select a cream #2 rectangle and two assorted print 1½" squares from the block-frame set. Join the pieces. Press. Repeat to piece a total of 24 sashing units measuring 1½" × 4½", including the seam allowances.

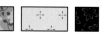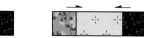

Make 24 units,
1½" × 4½".

2. Lay out four sashing units and three 1½" cream #2 squares end-to-end as shown. Join the pieces. Press. Repeat to piece a total of three sashing rows measuring 1½" × 19½", including the seam allowances. Reserve the remaining sashing units for later use.

Make 3 sashing rows,
1½" × 19½".

Double-Take Tip

THE SIMPLE THINGS IN LIFE

The Framed Pinwheel blocks in this little quilt can be modified and simplified to provide a new look, bringing a very different and charming feel to your project. Replacing the half-square triangles in the block corners with cream squares will speed the patchwork process, and this optional modification forms sweet little nine patches when the quilt top is assembled with the sashing units. If you choose this approach, simply reduce the number of 2" squares cut from each pinwheel patchwork set from four squares to two, and replace them with four 1½" squares from cream print #2 for the corners in each block.

Alternate layout

PIECING THE QUILT TOP

1. Lay out four Framed Pinwheel blocks and three sashing units in alternating positions. Join the pieces. Press. Repeat to piece four block rows measuring 4½" × 19½", including the seam allowances.

Make 4 block rows,
4½" × 19½".

2. Lay out the four block rows and the pieced sashing rows in alternating positions as shown. Join the rows. Press the seam allowances toward the sashing rows. The pieced quilt top should measure 19½" square.

Quilt assembly

COMPLETING THE QUILT

Layer and baste the quilt top, batting, and backing. Quilt the layers. The featured quilt is machine quilted with an edge-to-edge Baptist fan design. Join the dark print binding strips together to make one length and use it to bind the quilt.

Pin Point Tip

ZINGER PRINTS

To keep my mix of prints from looking too flat and bland, I often throw in what I consider to be a "zinger" or two. Zinger prints (such as the high-contrast navy-and-cream print I used for one of my Framed Pinwheel blocks and the binding) are those that stand out a bit from the others, but in a *good* way. Using a zinger print only once might look like an accident or a misstep in your fabric choices because it *is* different than the others, but using a zinger print two or three times across the top and spacing it at intervals will add sparkle and become the key to your success. With this approach, your choices will look intentional, create lots of visual interest, and provide a nice sense of balance!

Maple Stars

For this autumn-flavored patchwork throw, I began with the traditional Maple Leaf block and then double dipped it to drop a sweet little star right into the center of it. Alternating the direction of the blocks, along with a sprinkling of scrappy sashing stars and an occasional splash of sky blue, brings a great sense of movement and a rich, first-frost color palette to this quilt.

FINISHED QUILT SIZE: 62½" × 62½" | **FINISHED BLOCK SIZE: 10" × 10"**

MATERIALS

Yardage is based on a 42" width of useable fabric after prewashing and removing selvages.

25 assorted fat eighths (9" × 21"): 5 *each* of 5 colors (brown, green, orange, red, and gold) for maple leaf and star patchwork

⅔ yard of dark red print for star patchwork, border corner posts, and binding

3 assorted chubby sixteenths (9" × 10½") in shades of teal and aqua for star patchwork

1¾ yards of cream print for block backgrounds

1¾ yards of tan stripe or print for sashing strips and border

4 yards of fabric for backing

69" × 69" square of batting

CUTTING

Cut all pieces across the width of the fabric in the order given unless otherwise noted.

From *each* of the 5 brown prints, cut:

1 strip, 3" × 21"; subcut as follows:

- Cut a 6" length from the strip; from this 6" length, cut 1 square, 2⅞" × 2⅞". Cut the square in half diagonally *once* to yield 2 triangles.
- Cut the remaining 3" × 15" strip in half lengthwise to make 2 strips, 1½" × 15"; crosscut the strips into 16 squares, 1½" × 1½" (combined total of 80; extra squares will be used for the sashing stars)

2 strips, 2½" × 21"; crosscut into:

- 6 rectangles, 2½" × 4½" (combined total of 30)
- 2 squares, 2½" × 2½" (combined total of 10)
- 1 strip, 1¼" × 8" (combined total of 5)

Organize a 2½" square and 8 small (1½") squares from each of the 5 brown prints into brown star patchwork sets. Group the remaining pieces from the 5 brown prints into one brown maple leaf patchwork set.

From the green, red, gold, and orange prints:

Repeat the cutting listed for the brown prints for each of the 5 prints in each color; organize the pieces by color into the previously described star and maple leaf patchwork sets.

From the dark red print, cut:

7 strips, 2½" × 42". Crosscut *1* strip into 9 squares, 2½" × 2½"; reserve the remainder of this strip with the other 6 strips for binding.

2 strips, 1½" × 42"; crosscut into 48 squares, 1½" × 1½"

Organize 5 of the 2½" dark red squares with the 1½" dark red squares to make a dark red star patchwork set. Reserve the remaining 4 dark red 2½" squares for the border corner posts.

From *each* of the 3 teal and aqua prints, cut:

1 strip, 2½" × 10½"; crosscut into 2 squares, 2½" × 2½" (combined total of 5)

4 strips, 1½" × 10½"; crosscut into 24 squares, 1½" × 1½" (combined total of 72)

Organize each 2½" square with 8 matching 1½" squares into a teal star patchwork set. (You'll have extra 1½" squares to use for the sashing stars.)

From the cream print, cut:

2 strips, 2⅞" × 42"; crosscut into 25 squares, 2⅞" × 2⅞". Cut each square in half diagonally *once* to yield 2 triangles (combined total of 50)

11 strips, 2½" × 42"; crosscut into:

- 50 rectangles, 2½" × 4½"
- 175 squares, 2½" × 2½"

4 strips, 5" × 42"; crosscut into 25 squares, 5" × 5". Cut each square in half diagonally *once* to yield 2 triangles (combined total of 50).

From the tan stripe, cut:

22 strips, 2½" × 42"; crosscut *14* of the strips into 40 sashing strips, 2½" × 10½" (If you haven't prewashed your fabric, you may be able to cut four 10½" strips from each strip and reduce the number of strips needed from 14 to 10.)

Pin Point Tip

ADJUSTING THE VOLUME

When considering background prints for your projects, keep in mind that "busier" prints will have the effect of muting the look of your quilting stitches, making the stitching more of a background element of texture with just a subtle whisper of the stitched design. If you'd like your quilting stitches to make a stronger statement in your finished quilt and be more easily seen, simply turn down the "volume" of your background prints by choosing more tonal, muted designs. Taking this approach to choosing your background prints will turn *up* the volume of your quilting stitches.

Piecing the Maple Star Blocks

Sew all pieces with right sides together using a ¼" seam allowance unless otherwise noted. Press the seam allowances as indicated by the arrows or otherwise specified.

1. Select the pieces for one block as follows.

From the brown maple leaf patchwork set, choose:
- 6 rectangles, 2½" × 4½"
- 2 triangles cut from 2⅞" squares
- 1 strip, 1¼" × 8"
- 1 square, 2½" × 2½"

For a good blend of prints across the quilt top, I chose my pieces so that each of the five brown prints would be used twice per block. You can choose the prints for the patchwork pieces listed above in a completely random manner if you'd like.

From the cream print, choose:

- 7 squares, 2½" × 2½"
- 2 triangles cut from 2⅞" squares
- 2 triangles cut from 5" squares
- 2 rectangles, 2½" × 4½"

From a complementary color, choose:

1 star patchwork set in a complementary color consisting of 1 square, 2½" × 2½", and 8 squares, 1½" × 1½" Reserve the remaining pieces of the star patchwork set for other blocks.

2. Use a pencil and an acrylic ruler to draw a diagonal sewing line from corner to corner on the wrong side of six cream 2½" squares and the eight complementary color 1½" squares for star points. Reserve the prepared star-point squares for step 6. Layer a prepared cream square onto one end of a brown 2½" × 4½" rectangle as shown. Stitch the pair along the drawn line. Fold the resulting inner triangle open, aligning the corner with the corner of the brown rectangle. Press. Trim away the layers beneath the top triangle, leaving a ¼" seam allowance. Repeat to piece a total of three brown leaf-point units and three mirror-image brown leaf-point units measuring 2½" × 4½", including the seam allowances.

Make 3 of each unit,
2½" × 4½".

3. Join a cream and a brown 2⅞" triangle along the long diagonal edges. Press. Trim away dog-ear points. Repeat to piece a total of two brown half-square-triangle units measuring 2½" square, including the seam allowances.

Make 2 units,
2½" × 2½".

4. Fold the brown 1¼" × 8" strip in half crosswise and finger-press to crease the center. In the same manner,

fold the two cream 5" triangles in half and finger-press a center crease along each diagonal edge.

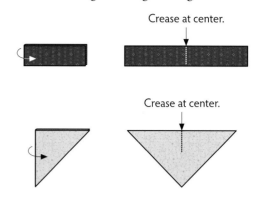

Crease at center.

Crease at center.

5. Align the crease of the brown strip with the crease of a cream triangle; join the pieces. Press. Repeat to join the second tan triangle to the remaining side of the brown strip. Press. Keeping the brown strip centered, use a rotary cutter and an acrylic ruler to trim the stem unit to 4½" square, including the seam allowances.

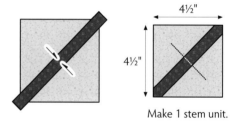

4½"

4½"

Make 1 stem unit.

6. Stitch a reserved prepared 1½" star-point square to the brown end of two leaf-point and mirror-image leaf-point units from step 2 as shown. These embellished leaf-point units should measure 2½" × 4½", including the seam allowances.

Make 2 units,
2½" × 4½".

Make 2 units,
2½" × 4½".

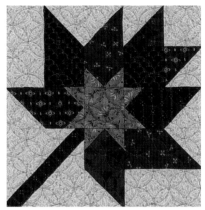

7. Lay out the two brown half-square-triangle units from step 3 with a brown and a tan 2½" square. Join the pieces in each horizontal row as shown. Press. Join the rows. Press. The pieced leaf-tip unit should measure 4½" square, including the seam allowances.

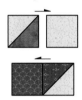

Make 1 leaf-tip unit, 4½" × 4½".

8. Lay out the leaf-tip unit with a leaf-point and a mirror-image leaf-point unit from step 6 and the complementary print 2½" square in two horizontal rows. Join the pieces in each row. Press. Join the rows. Press. The leaf corner unit should measure 6½" square, including the seam allowances.

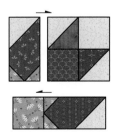
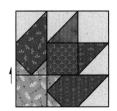

Make 1 corner unit, 6½" × 6½".

9. Lay out the remaining leaf-point and mirror-image leaf-point units from step 2, the remaining leaf-point and mirror-image embellished leaf-point units from

step 6, and two tan 2½" × 4½" rectangles as shown for a leaf-point and mirror-image leaf-point side units. Join the pieces in each unit in horizontal rows. Press. Join the rows. Press. The resulting units should measure 4½" × 6½", including the seam allowances.

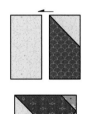
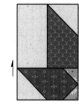
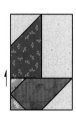

Make 1 of each unit, 4½" × 6½".

10. Lay out the side leaf-point and mirror-image side leaf-point units, the leaf corner unit from step 8, and the stem unit from step 5 in two horizontal rows. Join the pieces in each row. Press. Join the rows. Press. The pieced Maple Star block should measure 10½" square, including the seam allowances.

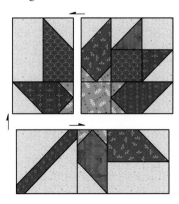

Make 1 Maple Star block, 10½" × 10½".

11. Repeat steps 1–10 to piece five Maple Star blocks in each colorway for a total of 25 blocks. From the star patchwork sets that remain, mingle all the 2½" star-center squares and the 1½" star-point squares into one combined sashing star patchwork set.

Piecing the Sashing Units

1. From the sashing-star patchwork set, choose two assorted print 1½" squares and prepare them by marking a diagonal sewing line as previously instructed. Layer a square onto one end of a tan stripe 2½" × 10½" strip and stitch, press, and trim as previously instructed. Repeat to piece a total of 16 sashing A units measuring 2½" × 10½", including the seam allowances.

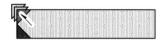

Make 16 sashing A units,
2½" × 10½".

2. Using a tan 2½" × 10½" strip and four assorted 1½" squares per unit, repeat step 1 to piece 24 sashing B units measuring 2½" × 10½", including the seam allowances. You'll have a handful of unused 1½" star-point squares after completing the sashing unit patchwork; these have been included for added choices as you stitch the units.

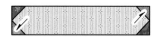

Make 24 sashing B units,
2½" × 10½".

Piecing the Quilt Center

For a good balance of color across the quilt center, I used one block from each of the five leaf colorways in each horizontal row. You can follow this guideline or choose your own color placement.

1. Lay out five Maple Star blocks and four sashing A units in alternate positions, with the blocks turned as shown. Join the pieces. Press. Block row A should measure 10½" × 58½", including the seam allowances.

Make 1 A row, 10½" × 58½".

2. Lay out five Maple Star blocks and four sashing B units in alternate positions, turning the blocks as shown. Join the pieces. Press. Repeat to piece two of block row B, measuring 10½" × 58½", including the seam allowances.

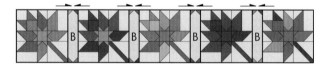

Make 2 B rows, 10½" × 58½".

3. Lay out five Maple Star blocks and four sashing B units in alternating positions, with the blocks turned as shown. Join the pieces. Press. Block row C should measure 10½" × 58½", including the seam allowances.

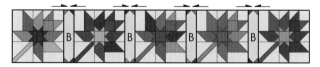

Make 1 C row, 10½" × 58½".

4. Lay out the five remaining Maple Star blocks and four sashing A units in alternating positions, turning the blocks as shown on page 72. Join the pieces and

Simple Double-Dipped Quilts

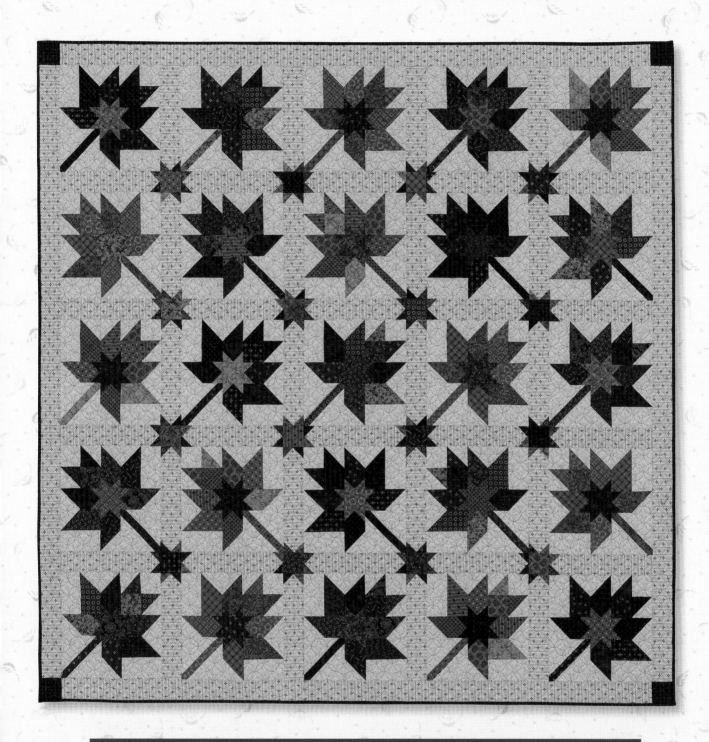

Designed by Kim Diehl. Pieced by Becky Marzano. Machine quilted by Connie Tabor.

Maple Stars

press. Block row D should measure 10½" × 58½", including the seam allowances.

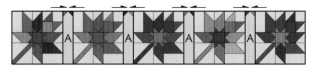

Make 1 D row, 10½" × 58½".

5. Lay out two sashing A units, three sashing B units, and four assorted 2½" star-center squares as shown. Join the pieces. Press. Repeat to piece a total of four sashing rows measuring 2½" × 58½", including the seam allowances.

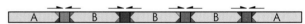

Make 4 sashing rows, 2½" × 58½".

6. Referring to the illustration, lay out the block and sashing rows to form the quilt center. Join the rows. Press the seam allowances toward the sashing rows. The pieced quilt center should measure 58½" square, including the seam allowances.

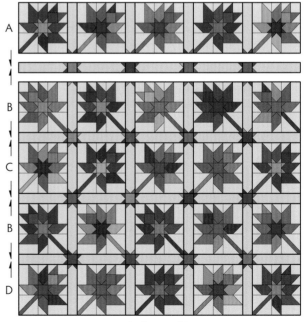

Quilt assembly

ADDING THE BORDER

1. Fold each side of the quilt center in half to determine the middle position and finger-press a center crease at the edge.

2. Join the eight tan stripe 42"-long strips in pairs to make four long border strips. Press the seam allowances to one side.

3. Lining up the center crease with the center seam of the pieced sashing strip, join a border strip to the right and left sides of the quilt center. Trim away the excess strip lengths on each side of the quilt top so they are 58½". Press the seam allowances toward the sashing strips.

4. Measuring 29¼" from each side of the center seam, trim the remaining pieced sashing strips to 58½" in length. (You may wish to measure the remaining quilt center sides to ensure the mathematically correct length fits the quilt top well, making an adjustment to the lengths if needed.) Join a dark red 2½" corner square to each end of the prepared border strips. Press the seam allowances toward the border. Join these border strips to the top and bottom edges of the quilt top. Press the seam allowances toward the sashing strips.

COMPLETING THE QUILT

Layer and baste the quilt top, batting, and backing. Quilt the layers. The featured quilt is machine quilted with an edge-to-edge intersecting orange peel design. Join the dark red binding strips together to make one length and use it to bind the quilt.

Double-Take Tip

TAKING A SHORTCUT TO COZY STYLE

Are you short on time but still in the mood to stitch an autumn-themed quilt? If so, consider stitching a bed runner in place of a larger lap-sized quilt! Simply follow the project directions to piece just 12 blocks. Join the blocks as shown, including the pieced sashing units, to complete the scrappy sashing stars between the blocks. Use two pieced outer-border sashing strips measuring 70½" in length for each long side of the runner and a 22½"-long strip for each short end, add the corner posts, and you're done! Layer your patchwork runner over a wholecloth quilt, add throw pillows if you'd like, and then grab your favorite book, beverage, and wooly socks for some comfy me time.

Bed-runner layout

Maple Stars

Surprise Inside

Double dipping the traditional Orange Peel design was a must-do for me, because it was an opportunity to enhance a very basic appliqué shape with the surprise element of a pieced Nine Patch center. Already iconic and classic on their own, each component shines more brightly when combined to make one beautifully blended block.

FINISHED QUILT SIZE: 28½" × 28½" | FINISHED BLOCK SIZE: 4" × 4"

MATERIALS

Yardage is based on a 42" width of useable fabric after prewashing and removing selvages. Keep in mind that the assorted dark prints called for below will be resting against a black background so the majority of them shouldn't be overly dark.

1 yard of subtle black print for pieced and appliquéd blocks

¼ yard (not a fat quarter) of cream print for patchwork

12 bitty bricks (4½" × 10½") of assorted prints for appliqué and binding

38 charm squares (5" × 5") or equivalent scraps for appliqué and binding

Supplies for your favorite appliqué method, including freezer paper for making a pattern template

Liquid fabric seam sealant (such as Fray Check) is suggested, but optional

1 yard of fabric for backing

33" × 33" square of batting

CUTTING

Cut all pieces across the width of the fabric in the order given unless otherwise noted. Instructions for cutting the appliqués are provided separately on page 77.

From the black print, cut:

4 strips, 1" × 42"

6 strips, 1¾" × 42"; crosscut into 48 rectangles, 1¾" × 4½"

2 strips, 2" × 42"; crosscut at 1¾" intervals to yield 46 rectangles, 2" × 1¾". **Note:** If you don't prewash your fabrics, the length of your strips may allow you to cut an additional rectangle from each strip for a total of 48.

3 strips, 4½" × 42"; crosscut into 25 squares, 4½" × 4½". (If you only cut 46 rectangles, 2" × 1¾", above, then cut 2 additional rectangles from the remainder of the 4½" strips for a total of 48.)

From the cream print, cut:

5 strips, 1" × 42"

From the assorted bitty bricks and charm squares or scraps, cut:

Enough 2½"-wide random-length pieces to make a 124" length of binding when joined together end to end. (For my chubby-binding method provided on page 103, reduce the width of the pieces to 2".)

Reserve the scraps of all bitty bricks and charm squares for the appliqués.

PIECING THE NINE PATCH BLOCKS

Sew all pieces with right sides together using a ¼" seam allowance unless otherwise noted. Press the seam allowances as indicated by the arrows or otherwise specified.

1. Join one black and two cream 1" × 42" strips along the long edges to make strip set A. Press. Repeat to piece a total of two A strip sets. Crosscut the strip sets at 1" intervals to yield a total of 48 strip set A units measuring 1" × 2", including the seam allowances.

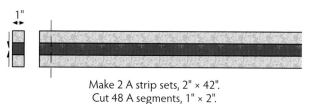

Make 2 A strip sets, 2" × 42".
Cut 48 A segments, 1" × 2".

2. Join the remaining cream and two black strips along the long edges to make strip set B. Press. Crosscut the strip set at 1" intervals to yield a total of 24 strip set B units measuring 1" × 2", including the seam allowances.

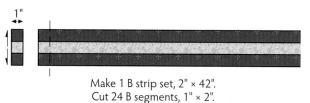

Make 1 B strip set, 2" × 42".
Cut 24 B segments, 1" × 2".

3. Join two strip set A units and one strip set B unit to make a nine-patch unit. Press. Repeat to piece a total of 24 nine-patch units measuring 2" square, including the seam allowances.

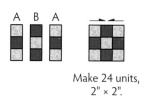

Make 24 units,
2" × 2".

4. Join black 2" × 1¾" rectangles to the right and left sides of a nine-patch unit. Press. Repeat to piece a total of 24 nine-patch rectangle units measuring 2" × 4½", including the seam allowances.

Make 24 units,
2" × 4½".

5. Join black 1¾" × 4½" rectangles to the top and bottom edges of a nine-patch rectangle unit. Press. Repeat to piece a total of 24 Nine Patch blocks to serve as foundation squares for the Orange Blossom blocks, 4½" × 4½", including the seam allowances.

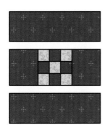
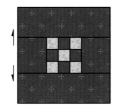

Make 24 blocks,
4½" × 4½".

APPLIQUÉING THE ORANGE BLOSSOM BLOCKS

The orange peel appliqué pattern is provided on page 81. Use freezer paper and refer to "Preparing Pattern Tracing Templates" on page 97 to make a pattern tracing template, or substitute your own favorite method, for the steps that follow.

I recommend applying a thin line of liquid seam sealant around the edges of each Nine Patch block to preserve the seam allowances and protect them from fraying as they're being handled during the appliqué steps, but this is entirely up to you!

1. Fold each Nine Patch block in half vertically, with right sides together, and use a hot, dry iron to lightly press a center crease. In the same manner, refold each block in half horizontally and lightly press the center position to form a creased plus sign.

Press creases to
mark block centers.

2. Referring to "Kim's Invisible Machine Appliqué" on page 97, or substituting your own favorite method,

Pin Point Tip

FUSSY CUTTING FOR THE WIN

When I'm preparing shapes for invisible machine appliqué, I've learned that "fussy cutting" to highlight a specific element of any given print (such as small surprises like the bird and rabbit shown above) can really add to the look of the finished appliqués. And it's easy to do! After attaching my freezer-paper pattern piece to the wrong side of the print with a small dab of fabric glue stick on the dull side of the paper, I turn the fabric to the front and hold it in front of a window or light box. The light creates a shadow of the pattern piece so I can see where it's resting on the print, letting me know exactly how the print will appear on my finished appliqué. If I don't like the placement, or if I'm missing a portion of the print that I'd really like to include, I reposition the pattern piece for a better result.

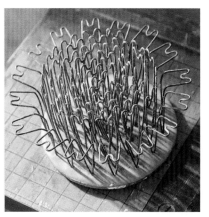

use the prepared pattern tracing template and the reserved assorted prints and scraps to prepare 200 orange peel appliqués.

3. Choose four assorted orange peel appliqués and a creased Nine Patch block. Position an appliqué diagonally onto one corner of the block, with the points resting on the pressed plus-sign creases, two or three threads in from where the ¼" seamline will fall when the quilt top is assembled. Repeat with the remaining three appliqués to create the circular orange peel design. When you're pleased with the placement and ensure everything fits well, baste or pin the appliqués in place (my glue-basting technique on page 100 works perfectly to anchor the appliqués firmly to the background so they don't shift during the stitching step). Repeat with the remaining Nine Patch blocks and prepared appliqués to baste a total of 24 Orange Blossom blocks.

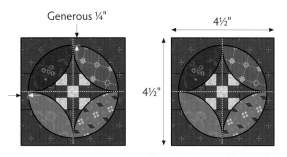

Baste 24 Orange Blossom blocks.

4. Use your favorite method to appliqué the 24 Orange Blossom blocks. If you plan to machine appliqué these blocks, I've shared the continuous stitching path that I used when stitching my own project; following this path will eliminate the need for a lot of starts and stops as you stitch.

Appliqué stitching path beginning at the white dot.

APPLIQUÉING THE ORANGE PEEL BLOCKS

Repeat steps 1–4 of "Appliquéing the Orange Blossom Blocks" using the black 4½" squares and the remaining prepared appliqués. Stitch a total of 25 appliquéd Orange Peel blocks. You'll have four unused Orange Peel appliqués; these have been included for added choices as you lay out the blocks.

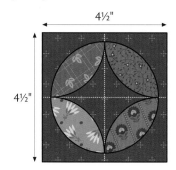

Appliqué 25 Orange Peel blocks.

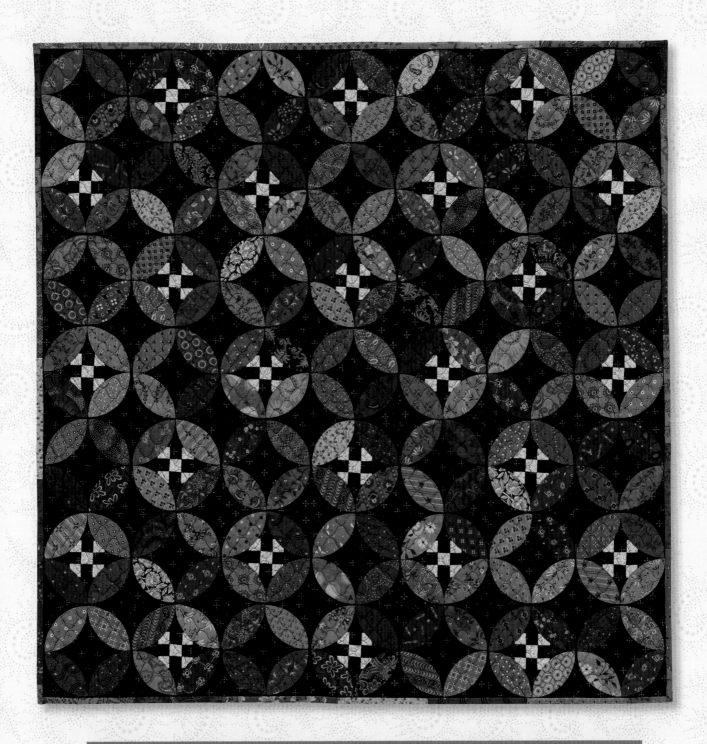

Designed, pieced, and appliquéd by Kim Diehl. Machine quilted by Connie Tabor.

Double-Take Tip

HERE A TWEAK, THERE A TWEAK

With a simple tweak or two, this Surprise Inside quilt design can bring lots of options to the table for very different finished looks. Try reversing the placement of the black and cream fabrics in the Nine Patches for a lighter quilt, or even consider treating the number of appliquéd blocks with nine-patch centers as a fluid concept, changing the number used and rearranging them from the original layout of to create new secondary patterns. Finally, think about using a light version of your favorite color for the background print (such as aqua or apple green), and complete your design using appliqués fashioned from complementary colors.

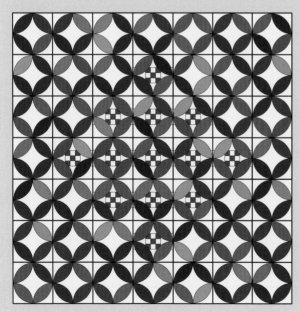

Alternate layout

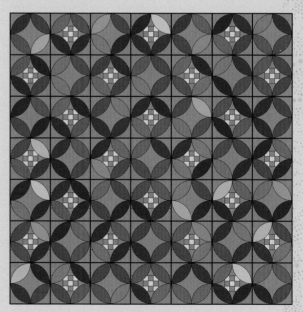

Alternate colorway

PIECING THE QUILT TOP

1. Select four Orange Peel blocks and three Orange Blossom blocks. Lay out the blocks side by side in alternating positions. Join the blocks to piece an A row. Press. Repeat to piece a total of four A rows measuring 4½" × 28½", including the seam allowances.

Make 4 A rows,
4½" × 28½".

2. Select four Orange Blossom blocks and three Orange Peel blocks. Lay out the blocks side by side in alternating positions. Join the blocks to piece a B row. Press. Repeat to piece a total of three B rows measuring 4½" × 28½", including the seam allowances.

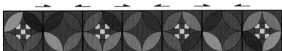

Make 3 B rows,
4½" × 28½".

3. Referring to the quilt assembly diagram below, lay out the pieced A and B rows in alternating positions. Join the rows. Press the seam allowances toward the A rows. The pieced quilt top should measure 28½" square.

COMPLETING THE QUILT

Layer and baste the quilt top, batting, and backing. Quilt the layers. The featured quilt is stitched with an edge-to-edge chicken-wire design. Join the 2½"-wide random lengths of assorted prints to make one strip, and use it to bind the quilt.

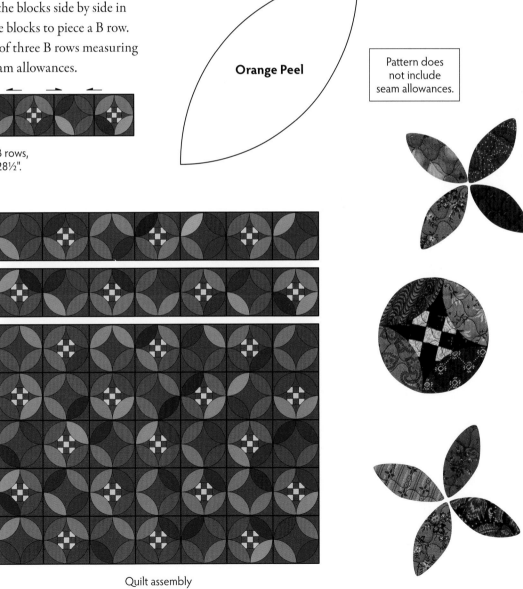

Orange Peel

Pattern does not include seam allowances.

Quilt assembly

Surprise Inside   81

Heritage Blossoms

Often when I'm working on a block design, I start at the center and work my way outward. For the double-dipped blocks in this quilt, I changed things up and began with a sweet little pieced blossom in each corner, and then worked my way inward *to create the illusion that they were blooming from a starburst frame filled with classic patchwork. The result? Floral fireworks!*

FINISHED QUILT SIZE: 76½" × 76½" | **FINISHED BLOCK SIZE: 20" × 20"**

MATERIALS

Yardage is based on a 42" width of useable fabric after prewashing and removing selvages.

⅞ yard of black print for center Star Blossom block, pieced border, and binding

⅝ yard of gray print for center Star Blossom block and border #2

2 yards of cream print #1 for Star Blossom blocks and pieced border

3 yards of cream print #2 for Star Blossom blocks

8 fat eighths (9" × 21") of assorted dark prints for Star Blossom blocks

8 fat quarters (18" × 21") of assorted medium prints for Star Blossom blocks and pieced border. **Note:** each fat eighth should be a lighter shade of a color included in the dark prints above.

1 yard of cream print #3 for sashing units and border #1

14 squares, 6" × 6", of assorted prints for pieced border

2⅓ yards of 108"-wide fabric *OR* 4⅔ yards of 42"-wide fabric for backing

83" × 83" square of batting

CUTTING

Cut all pieces across the width of the fabric in the order given unless otherwise noted.

From the black print, cut:

1 strip, 5½" × 42"; crosscut into 2 squares, 5½" × 5½". Cut each square in half diagonally *twice* to yield 4 triangles (combined total of 8).

From the remainder of the strip, cut 2 strips, 2½" wide; from these strips, cut:
- 17 squares, 2½" × 2½"
- 8 squares, 1½" × 1½"

Keep all pieces cut above organized into a black star-blossom unit set.

8 binding strips, 2½" × 42". (For my chubby-binding technique provided on page 103, reduce the strip width to 2".)

From the gray print, cut:

1 strip, 1½" × 42"; crosscut into 1 strip, 1½" × 21"

1 strip, 2½" × 42"; crosscut into 16 squares, 2½" × 2½"

1 strip, 3" × 42"; crosscut into:
- 6 squares, 3" × 3". Cut each square in half diagonally *once* to yield 2 triangles (combined total of 12).
- 4 squares, 2½" × 2½" (combined total of 20 with the previously cut squares).

Add all the above gray pieces to the black star-blossom unit set.

8 strips, 1½" × 42", for border #2

From cream print #1, cut:

4 strips, 5½" × 42"; crosscut into:
- 25 squares, 5½" × 5½". Cut each square in half diagonally *twice* to yield 4 triangles (combined total of 100).
- 4 rectangles, 1½" × 2½" (combined total of 36 with previously cut rectangles).

1 strip, 4½" × 42"; crosscut into 4 squares, 4½" × 4½"

9 strips, 2½" × 42"; crosscut into 72 rectangles, 2½" × 4½"

8 strips, 1½" × 42"; crosscut into:
- 10 strips, 1½" × 21"
- 32 rectangles, 1½" × 2½"
- 36 squares, 1½" × 1½"

From cream print #2, cut:

2 strips, 5½" × 42"; crosscut into 9 squares, 5½" × 5½". Cut each square in half diagonally *twice* to yield 4 triangles (combined total of 36). From the remainder of the last strip, cut 2 strips, 2½" wide; crosscut into 12 rectangles, 2½" × 4½".

27 strips, 2½" × 42"; crosscut into:
- 36 rectangles, 2½" × 8½"
- 132 rectangles, 2½" × 4½" (combined total of 144 with previously cut rectangles).
- 72 squares, 2½" × 2½"

5 strips, 3" × 42"; crosscut into 54 squares, 3" × 3". Cut each square in half diagonally *once* to yield 2 triangles (combined total of 108).

From *each* of the dark-print fat eighths, cut:

1 strip, 5½" × 21"; crosscut into:
- 2 squares, 5½" × 5½" (combined total of 16). Cut each square in half diagonally *twice* to yield 4 triangles (total of 8, combined total of 64).
- From the remainder of the strip, cut 2 strips, 2½" × 10"; crosscut into 6 squares, 2½" × 2½" (combined total of 48).

1 strip, 2½" × 21"; crosscut into 3 squares, 2½" × 2½" (combined total of 72 with previously cut squares). From the remainder of the strip, cut 8 squares, 1½" × 1½" (combined total of 64).

Organize the pieces cut from each fat eighth into a starburst side-unit set.

From *each* of the 8 medium fat quarters, cut:

1 strip, 5½" × 21"; from 1 end of this strip, cut 4 squares, 2½" × 2½" (combined total of 32). Reserve the remainder of each medium assorted print 5½" strip for use in border #3.

1 strip, 3" × 21"; crosscut into 6 squares, 3" × 3" (combined total of 48). Cut each square in half diagonally *once* to yield 2 triangles (combined total of 96).

3 strips, 2½" × 21"; crosscut into 17 squares, 2½" × 2½" (combined total of 168 with previously cut squares)

1 strip, 1½" × 21" (combined total of 8)

Organize the pieces above by print, adding each group to its coordinating dark star-blossom set.

From the remainder of the assorted medium 5½" strips, cut a *combined total* of:

16 squares, 5½" × 5½"; cut each square in half diagonally *twice* to yield 4 triangles (combined total of 64). **Note:** For an even scrappier border, you can incorporate additional prints from your stash as I did when cutting some of the pieces for the hourglass patchwork and the triangle patchwork set that follows.

Keep the triangles organized into a pieced border patchwork set.

From cream print #3, cut:

7 strips, 2½" × 42"; crosscut 3 of the strips into 6 sashing strips, 2½" × 20½". Reserve the remaining 2½"-wide strips for use as the quilt center is pieced.

8 strips, 1½" × 42"

From *each* of the 6" squares of assorted prints, cut:

4 squares, 2½" × 2½" (combined total of 56)

Add the assorted print squares to the pieced border patchwork set.

PIECING THE STAR BLOSSOM BLOCKS

Sew all pieces with right sides together using a ¼" seam allowance unless otherwise noted. Press the seam allowances as indicated by the arrows or otherwise specified.

1. Select the black Star Blossom patchwork set. To this set, add cream #1 and cream # 2 pieces, as follows:

Cream #1:

- 4 rectangles, 1½" × 2½"
- 4 squares, 1½" × 1½"
- 1 strip, 1½" × 21"
- 4 triangles cut from 5½" squares

Cream #2:

- 12 triangles cut from 3" squares
- 4 triangles cut from 5½" squares
- 16 rectangles, 2½" × 4½"
- 8 squares, 2½" × 2½"
- 4 rectangles, 2½" × 8½"

2. Use a pencil and an acrylic ruler to draw a diagonal sewing line from corner to corner on the wrong side of each black 1½" square. Layer a prepared square onto one end of a cream 1½" × 2½" rectangle. Stitch the pair along the drawn line. Fold the resulting inner black triangle open, aligning the corner with the corner of the cream rectangle. Press. Trim away the layers beneath the top triangle, leaving a ¼" seam allowance. In the same manner, add a mirror-image triangle to the remaining end of the rectangle. Repeat to piece a total of four star-point units measuring 1½" × 2½", including the seam allowances.

Make 4 units,
1½" × 2½".

3. Lay out the four star-point units, four cream #1 squares, and one black 2½" square in three horizontal rows as shown. Join the pieces in each row. Press. Join the rows. Press. The pieced center-star unit should measure 4½" square, including the seam allowances.

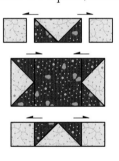 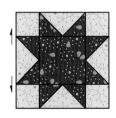

Make 1 center-star unit,
4½" × 4½".

4. Join the cream and gray 1½" × 21" strips along the long edges. Press. Crosscut the strip set into four strip-set units measuring 2½" × 4½", including the seam allowances.

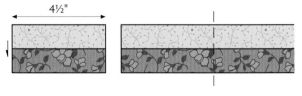

Make 1 strip set, 2½" × 21".
Cut 4 segments, 2½" × 4½".

5. Join a cream #2 and a gray triangle along the long diagonal edges. Press. Repeat to piece a total of four cream/gray half-square-triangle units. Trim each pieced unit to 2½" square, removing the dog-ear points in the process.

Make 4 units.

6. Lay out the center-star unit from step 3, the four strip-set units from step 4, and the four units from step 5 in three horizontal rows as shown. Join the pieces in each row. Press. Join the rows. Press. The pieced churn-dash-star unit should measure 8½" square, including the seam allowances.

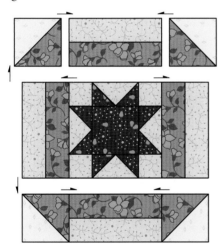

Make churn-dash-star unit, 8½" × 8½".

7. Join a black and a cream #2 triangle cut from 5½" squares along their short edges. Press. Repeat to piece a total of four cream #2 units. Repeat using four black and four cream #1 triangles cut from 5½" squares to piece a total of four cream #1 units.

Make 4 of each unit.

8. Join cream #1 and cream #2 triangle units from step 7 to piece an hourglass unit. Repeat to piece a total of four hourglass units. Trim each unit to 4½" square, removing the dog-ear points in the process.

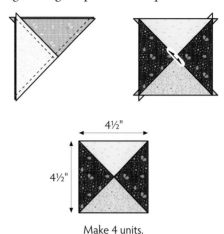

Make 4 units.

9. Referring to the stitch-and-fold method in step 2 on page 86, make four star-point units and four mirror-image star-point units using cream #2 rectangles and black 2½" squares. The pieced units should measure 2½" × 4½", including the seam allowances.

Make 4 of each unit, 2½" × 4½".

10. Join a pieced rectangle and a mirror-image pieced rectangle to opposite sides of an hourglass unit. Press. Repeat to piece a total of four units measuring 4½" × 8½", including the seam allowances.

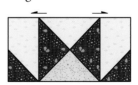

Make 4 units, 4½" × 8½".

11. Join a 2½" × 8½" cream #2 rectangle to the top edge of the hourglass unit. Press. Repeat to piece a total of four starburst side units measuring 6½" × 8½", including the seam allowances.

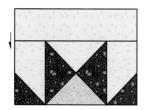

Make 4 units,
6½" × 8½".

12. Repeat step 2 using 16 gray 2½" squares and eight 2½" × 4½" cream #2 rectangles to piece a total of eight blossom-point units measuring 2½" × 4½", including the seam allowances.

Make 8 units,
2½" × 4½".

13. Using eight gray and eight cream #2 triangles cut from 3" squares, repeat step 5 to piece a total of eight half-square-triangles measuring 2½" square, including the seam allowances.

2½"

2½"

Make 8 units.

14. Lay out two half-square-triangles, one gray 2½" square, and one cream #2 square in two horizontal rows as shown. Join the pieces in each row. Press. Join the rows. Press. Repeat to piece a total of four blossom-center units measuring 4½" square, including the seam allowances.

Make 4 units,
4½" × 4½".

15. Lay out the blossom-center unit, two blossom-point units from step 12, and one 2½" cream #2 square in two horizontal rows as shown. Join the pieces in each row. Press. Join the rows. Press. Repeat to piece a total of four blossom-corner units measuring 6½" square, including the seam allowances.

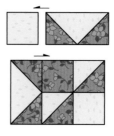 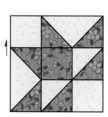

Make 4 units,
6½" × 6½".

16. Lay out the four pieced corner-blossom units, the four pieced starburst side units from step 11, and the pieced churn-dash-star unit from step 6 in three horizontal rows. Join the units. Press. Join the rows. Press. The pieced Star Blossom block should measure 20½" square, including the seam allowances.

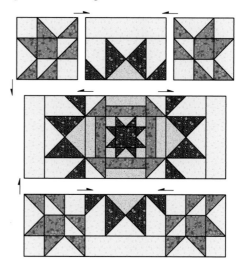

Make 1 Star Blossom block,
20½" × 20½".

17. Using the remaining eight starburst patchwork sets, repeat steps 1–16 to piece a total of nine Star Blossom blocks. Add the eight black 2½" squares remaining from the black star-blossom set to the pieced border patchwork set.

Simple Double-Dipped Quilts

DIVIDE AND CONQUER!

the center black Star Blossom block. (Having a completed block will help familiarize you with the patchwork steps and give you an easy reference for layout and pressing as you stitch the remaining blocks.)

Working on the blocks one horizontal row at a time, here's a quick summary of my partial piecing steps:

- Use steps 2–3 from the project directions to choose, prep, and stitch the pieces needed for the star units of *each* block in the chosen row. Lay out the pieced units in layers and complete the center-star units.

- Follow steps 4–6 to piece the churn-dash portions of the blocks, and then use the completed star units to finish the churn-dash-star units.

- Refer to steps 7–11 to piece the starburst side units.

- Follow steps 12–15 to complete the corner-blossom units.

- Lay out the partially pieced block components from the previous steps, stacking them in layers, and refer to step 16 to complete the blocks in the chosen row.

Complete steps for piecing the Star Blossom blocks are provided in this section, and they'll enable you to systematically stitch each block from start to finish. However, for quilts such as this with several pieced units included within each block, I sometimes divide and conquer the patchwork and take a partial-piecing approach. This means that I tackle the individual patchwork units in each block (such as the stars and blossoms) in batches of three or more blocks at a time to speed my progress.

For this project, I used a serving platter to organize the patchwork pieces into block sets as called for in "Cutting" on page 84, and then pieced

I've found that this approach to constructing the units for each block helps keep the patchwork organized and streamlined, and it's a great time-saver!

Piecing the Quilt Center

1. Lay out three Star Blossom blocks and two 2½" × 20½" cream #3 strips in alternating positions. Join the pieces. Press. Repeat to piece a total of three block rows (placing the black Star Blossom block as the center block of one row) measuring 20½" × 64½", including the seam allowances.

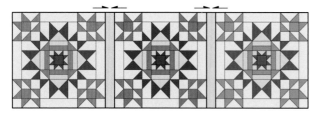

Make 3 rows, 20½" × 64½".

2. Join two 2½" × 42" cream #3 strips end to end to make one length. Press the seam allowances to one side. Repeat to make two pieced sashing strips. Trim each strip to 64½" long.

3. Referring to the assembly diagram, lay out the two pieced sashing strips and the three block rows from step 1 in five horizontal rows to form the quilt center. Join the rows. Press. The pieced quilt center should measure 64½" square, including the seam allowances.

Quilt assembly

Adding Borders #1 and #2

1. Join the eight 1½" × 42" cream #3 strips end to end in pairs. Press the seam allowances to one side.

2. Trim two of the border strips to 64½" long and sew them to the right and left sides of the quilt center.

3. Trim the remaining two borders to 66½" long and sew them to the top and bottom of the quilt center. The quilt top should measure 66½" square, including the seam allowances.

4. Repeat steps 1–3 using the eight gray 1½" × 42" strips to add border #2. The side borders should be trimmed to 66½" long, and the top and bottom borders should be 68½" long. The quilt top, including border #2, should now measure 68½" square, including the seam allowances.

Adding the Patchwork Border

1. Select the pieced border patchwork set, all of the cream #1 triangles cut from 5½" squares, and all of the 2½" × 4½" cream #1 rectangles.

2. From the patchwork set, select the assorted medium print triangles cut from 5½" squares. Join each print triangle to a cream #1 triangle to piece a total of 64 triangle units.

Make 64 units.

Designed and pieced by Kim Diehl. Machine quilted by Connie Tabor.

3. Join two triangle units to piece an hourglass unit. Press. Repeat to piece a total of 32 hourglass units. Trim each unit to 4½" square, removing the dog-ear points in the process.

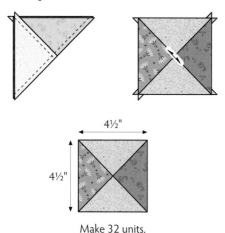

Make 32 units.

4. Select all the assorted print 2½" squares from the patchwork border set and the 2½" × 4½" cream #1 rectangles. Referring to step 2 of "Piecing the Star Blossom Blocks" on page 86, mark the print 2½" squares as previously instructed and follow the "stitch-and-fold" star-point technique to stitch a total of 36 pieced rectangles and 36 pieced mirror-image rectangles measuring 2½" × 4½", including the seam allowances.

Make 36 of each unit,
2½" × 4½".

Double-Take Tip

COLOR OPTIONS

It's always fascinated me that you can give 10 different people the very same quilt pattern and they'll make 10 very different-looking quilts. That's the fun of quiltmaking! Since I've never met a scrappy quilt I didn't like, I naturally chose to stitch my Heritage Blossoms project using a variety of richly hued prints. But I have to admit that the idea of approaching this design in a more planned, classic way was equally tempting to me—and it might be the perfect option for you!

If so, consider choosing two favorite colors for your design, such as the gray and cheddar option shown, top right, using just a single print from each color for a timeless and elegant look. Or, for a more modern take on tradition, channel the look of the teal and apple-green quilt, bottom right, keeping your background print clean and bright and incorporating a handful of prints in each of your two chosen colors for patchwork that looks crisp and fresh.

Alternate colorway

Alternate colorway

Simple Double-Dipped Quilts

5. Join a pieced rectangle and a pieced mirror-image rectangle to opposite sides of an hourglass unit from step 3 as shown. Press. Repeat to piece a total of 32 patchwork border units measuring 4½" × 8½", including the seam allowances. You will have four pieced rectangles and four pieced mirror-image rectangles left over to use in step 6.

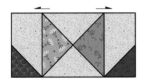

Make 32 units,
4½" × 8½".

6. Join eight pathwork border units end to end to make a pieced strip. Press. Repeat to piece a total of four pieced border strips that measure 4½" × 64½". Add a pieced rectangle to one end and a mirror-image pieced rectangle to the opposite end of each border strip so they measure 4½" × 68½", including the seam allowances. Press the seam allowances to one side in the direction that produces the best triangle points.

Make 4 borders,
4½" × 68½".

7. Referring to the adding borders diagram, above right, join a patchwork border strip to the right and left sides of the quilt top. Press. Join a 4½" cream #1 square to each end of the remaining two patchwork border

strips. Press the seam allowances toward the cream squares. Join these strips to the remaining sides of the quilt top. Press. The completed quilt top should measure 76½" square.

Adding the borders

COMPLETING THE QUILT

Layer and baste the quilt top, batting, and backing. Quilt the layers. The featured quilt is machine quilted with a repeating edge-to-edge design of feathered clamshells in clusters of four, with each clamshell positioned in a different direction to produce a nondirectional look. Join the black binding strips to make one length and use it to bind the quilt.

Kim's Quiltmaking Basics

You'll find the basic information needed for quiltmaking in the section that follows, with the information and techniques provided in simple, approachable steps. For even more details, please visit ShopMartingale.com/HowtoQuilt, where you can download free illustrated guidelines.

CUTTING MULTIPLE PRINTS FOR SCRAPPY QUILTS

When a project calls for numerous prints to be cut, I've learned that I'll get the best and quickest results when I layer and prepare them on my pressing surface first. Here are the steps I use:

1. Choose up to six prints for the group to be cut, layering the first print onto the pressing surface. Give the cloth a light misting of Best Press (a starch alternative) or water and press it smooth and flat with a hot iron.

2. Continue layering, misting, and pressing each new print, roughly aligning the edges along one side and the bottom with the previously positioned print, to form a stack. This layering and pressing approach will help meld the fabric layers together for easier cutting with minimal shifting, and the misting step will give the fabric added body and a crisp texture for great piecing results.

   Note: If your mix of prints includes a stripe or a pronounced pattern, save and position it as the top layer of the stack. Adding these types of prints as the topmost layer will enable you to position the pressed stack well for cutting, producing cut patchwork pieces with lines that run straight and true.

3. Transfer the pressed stack to the cutting board, aligning the topmost print with the cutting grid to ensure the weave of the cloth and the direction of the print is positioned well, and make the specified cuts.

Pin Point Tip

SENSE OF DIRECTION

Cutting instructions for quilting projects typically specify that the pieces be cut from the width of the fabric, meaning that you cut across the fabric from selvage to selvage. For smaller precut pieces of fabric that may be missing the selvage edges, such as chubby sixteenths, charm squares, or scraps, the width of fabric direction may not be obvious. While it isn't crucial that squares be cut from the width of fabric because they're nondirectional, rectangles will produce better patchwork results when they're cut from the width of fabric because there'll be a small bit of give to the cloth along the length of the pieces.

Any easy way to tell the difference between the width and the length of a piece of cloth without selvage edges is to hold two opposite ends of the cloth and gently pull apart. If there's a bit of stretch when pulled, you've found the width of fabric! If there is no give to the cloth when pulled, rotate the piece and try this step again from the alternate direction—the direction with the most stretch will be the width of fabric. Taking a moment to determine the direction of the width and length of the cloth will help ensure your very best patchwork results.

PINNING

I encourage you to pin your patchwork at regular intervals, including all sewn seams. My best tip for pinning, which helps me achieve great results when piecing my own quilts, is to "pin weave" the last pin at the tail end of each patchwork unit, where the cloth can receive a lot of stress from handling and wiggle free. Pin weaving simply means to weave the point of the pin through the cloth *twice* as shown in the illustration, to keep it securely in place. For large or long patchwork units that include many pinned areas, I repeat the pin-weaving step at spaced intervals to keep them securely in place for stitching.

One of the biggest benefits of weaving the last pin in each unit is that you can lay your fingertip over the pinhead as the tail end of the patchwork feeds under the presser foot and help guide it through the sewing machine in a straight line to eliminate fishtailing.

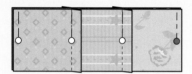

MACHINE PIECING

Unless the project directions specify otherwise, always join your fabrics with right sides together using a ¼" seam allowance. My personal preference is to use neutral-colored thread in both the needle and bobbin, rather than white thread, because neutral thread colors tend to blend better with a variety of prints and be less visible when the patchwork seams are pressed open.

Last, I recommend shortening your machine's stitch length slightly, even for larger scale patchwork projects, because this will produce secure seams from edge to edge with stitches that nestle into the cloth. For my sewing machine, I reduce the length from a standard setting of 2.2 down to 1.8.

PRESSING SEAMS

I'm often asked how I press my patchwork blocks because they lay beautifully flat and smooth when finished. Here are the steps I use:

1. Place the pieced unit on the pressing surface with the fabric you want to press *toward* positioned on top. Briefly bring your iron down onto the top layer of the unit at the seam to warm the cloth. While the fabric is still warm fold the top piece back to expose the seam and run your fingernail along the line of thread to open the cloth all the way to the seam.

2. Finish pressing the unit from the front to set the seams in place and smooth the fabric.

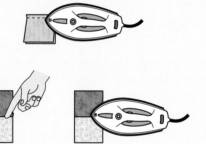

3. Once the block has been completed, this is where the magic really happens. Position the block *wrong* side up on the ironing surface and give it a light misting of Best Press (or water). Methodically work your way across the block to press the seams from the *back* to ensure they're laying smooth, flat, and (most importantly) in the intended direction. This approach will set the seams nicely in place and eliminate the sheen that can sometimes form on the front of the cloth from the iron.

Simple Double-Dipped Quilts

Kim's Invisible Machine Appliqué

For this appliqué method, you'll need the following supplies in addition to your standard sewing and quiltmaking items:

- .004 monofilament in smoke and clear colors
- Awl or stiletto with a sharp point
- Embroidery scissors with a sharp point
- Freezer paper
- Iron with a pronounced point for pressing shapes, with a nonstick surface if possible
- Fabric glue, in liquid and stick form, water-soluble and acid-free (my favorite brand is Quilter's Choice Basting Glue by Beacon Adhesives)
- Open-toe presser foot, or a foot with a clear acrylic center insert
- Pressing board with a firm surface
- Sewing machine with adjustable tension control, able to produce a zigzag stitch in a tiny size
- Size 75/11 (or smaller) machine-quilting needles
- Tweezers with a rounded tip

Preparing Pattern Tracing Templates

Keep in mind that only one template will be needed for any given appliqué shape, because it's simply a tool used to trace and cut the individual freezer-paper pattern pieces used to prepare the cloth appliqués for stitching. Here are the steps I use:

1. Cut a single piece of freezer paper, about twice as large as your shape. Lay the paper over the pattern sheet, waxy side down, and trace the shape onto one end.

2. Fold the traced paper in half, waxy sides together, and use a hot, dry iron to fuse the layers together.

3. Cut out the template shape exactly along the drawn line (the seam allowance will be added later).

Preparing Freezer-Paper Pattern Pieces

Pattern *pieces* are the individual paper shapes that will be used to prepare the cloth appliqués for stitching after the pattern *template* has been used to trace them. Here are the steps I use:

1. Use the pattern template (when many appliqués are needed) or trace directly from the pattern sheet (when only a handful of appliqués are needed) to transfer the shape onto one end of a strip of freezer paper, in a width that will accommodate the appliqué size.

2. Accordion fold the strip up to six layers deep (more than six layers will feel bulky and be difficult to cut).

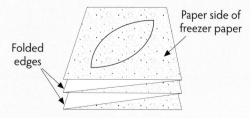

Folded edges

Paper side of freezer paper

3. Anchor the center of the shape with a straight pin or staple the paper in the background areas around the shape to stabilize the layers and prevent shifting. Cut out the shape exactly along the drawn line to produce up to six pattern pieces with each cut.

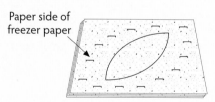

Paper side of freezer paper

4. Repeat steps 1–3 to make the number of shapes needed. Keep in mind that using the accordion-fold method outlined above for shapes that aren't perfectly symmetrical will produce mirror-image shapes from every other piece of freezer paper when the layers are separated. To make multiple identical nonsymmetrical shapes, simply replace the accordion-fold method with stacked individual layers of freezer paper, all positioned waxy side down.

Preparing the Appliqués from Fabric

1. Apply a small dab of fabric glue stick to the center of the nonwaxy side of the freezer-paper pattern piece and position it onto the wrong side of the fabric, *waxy side up.* When preparing more than one appliqué from a single piece of fabric, leave approximately ½" between the shapes.

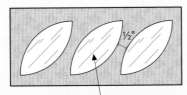

Wrong side of fabric, freezer paper waxy side up

2. Use embroidery scissors to cut out each shape, adding an approximate ¼" seam allowance. If this technique is new to you, a great visual aid to help you gauge the amount of seam allowance is to apply a piece of quarter-inch quilter's tape to your thumbnail on the hand that will be holding the appliqué as you cut the shape. Keep in mind that adding more than a ¼" seam allowance will produce extra bulk and make the seam allowance difficult to turn under and press in later steps.

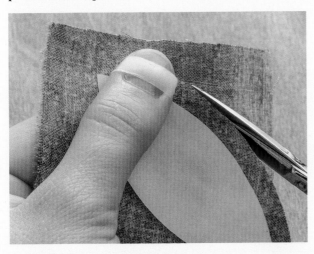

Pressing Fabric Appliqués

For the following steps, keep in mind that if you're right-handed you'll work from right to left as you prepare the shapes; if you're left-handed, reverse the direction and work from left to right.

1. Set your iron to the "cotton" setting, with no steam. Beginning at a straight edge or a gentle curve, *not* a corner, use your fingertip to smooth the fabric seam allowance over and onto the back of the appliqué so it's resting on the waxy surface of the freezer-paper pattern piece. As you slide your finger from the fabric toward the center of the shape away from the appliqué edge, immediately follow behind with the tip of your iron to fuse the fabric to the waxy surface of the pattern piece. Let the iron rest in place as you repeat to draw the next bit of seam-allowance fabric onto the pattern piece. (Letting the iron rest in place as described will add a couple additional seconds of heat, helping to ensure the fabric is firmly fused to the paper.)

Direct seam allowance toward center of shape.

2. As you approach the corner of the shape, fold the fabric seam allowance toward the back of the piece so it extends beyond the pattern point as shown, keeping the fabric snugged up against the paper edge. Press this first fold at the corner of the shape. Fold over the seam allowance on the remaining side of the point and continue pressing to complete the piece.

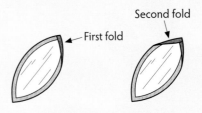

First fold

Second fold

3. Apply a small dab of fabric glue stick under the flap of the fabric seam allowance fold at each point. Use the tip of a sharp awl to grab and drag the fabric in and away from the appliqué edge so it will be hidden from the front of the shape. Use the point of the iron to fuse the seam allowance in place, removing the awl as the fabric is pressed.

Basting Appliqués

After laying out your appliqué design to ensure the pieces fit well and are positioned to your liking, you have the option of pinning them, thread basting them, *or* using my preferred method of glue basting. Glue basting keeps the shapes securely anchored in place, prevents shifting, and eliminates the shrinkage that can sometimes occur to the background of the block as the appliqués are stitched. Here are the glue-basting steps I use:

1. Choose an appliqué positioned in your layout. Without removing the shape from where it's resting on the background, fold back one half of the appliqué to expose the back of the piece, making the pressed seam allowance visible. Apply small dots of liquid fabric glue at approximately ½" intervals along the seam-allowance fabric around the exposed half of the appliqué, making sure to place a dot of glue on any points. Reposition the glue-basted half of the appliqué back onto the fabric, pressing it firmly in place with your hand, and repeat with the remaining half of the shape.

2. Once all of the shapes have been glue basted, use a hot, dry iron from the back of the block to heat set the glue dots and firmly anchor the appliqués to the fabric.

Preparing Your Sewing Machine

1. Insert a size 75/11 or smaller needle into the sewing machine and thread it with monofilament thread, choosing the smoke color for medium and dark prints or the clear color for lighter, brighter prints.

2. Wind the bobbin with neutral-colored all-purpose thread in a sturdy, not fine, weight. Heavier thread is the best choice because it will be more likely to remain on the wrong side of the block and resist pulling up through the weave of the fabric to the surface; fine thread can tend to slide up through the layers more easily and make your stitches visible. I also suggest avoiding prewound bobbins, as they can make it difficult to regulate the thread tension and achieve secure, invisible stitches.

Note: If your sewing machine's bobbin case features a "finger" with a special eye for use with embroidery techniques, threading your bobbin thread through this opening will help further regulate the tension and produce ideal stitches.

3. Set the sewing machine to the zigzag stitch and adjust the width and length settings to achieve a tiny stitch as shown below. Next, reduce the tension setting (a level of 1–2 for most machines) until the stitches on a test piece are sturdy and secure, with the bobbin thread remaining underneath the top layer of the piece and no visible bobbin-thread dots.

Approximate stitch size

STITCHING THE APPLIQUÉS

When time permits, I love hand stitching my appliqués, and at this point in the process you can still make this choice using a needle and matching thread in a fine weight. Once stitched, refer to "Removing Paper Pattern Pieces" on page 102 to complete the project.

For projects where my goal is to finish quickly, machine stitching the appliqués is my go-to choice because it produces invisibly stitched, sturdy appliqués in a fraction of the time needed for hand stitching. Here are the steps I use:

1. Slide the basted block under the presser foot from front to back (to direct the threads behind the machine), with the needle poised above the appliqué you plan to stitch. With the appliqué positioned to the left of the needle at a straight or gently curved edge, not a corner or point, drop the needle down into the appliqué, a few threads in from the edge. Grab the threads from the needle and bobbin behind the presser foot or lay your fingertip securely over them to prevent them from pulling up into the sewing machine and begin stitching.

2. Take two or three stitches, release the threads, and then begin stitching the perimeter of the appliqué; stop and clip the top thread after about an inch of the appliqué has been sewn. As you continue working your way around the appliqué, train your eyes to watch the outer stitches, ensuring they drop into the background exactly next to the appliqué, and the inner stitches will automatically fall inside the shape where they should.

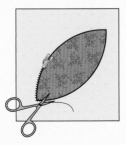

3. As you approach the point of the appliqué, stitch to the position where the outer stitch lands exactly next to the point and drops into the background and stop. Pivot the block and continue stitching along the remainder of the shape, overlapping your starting point by approximately ¼". If your machine offers this feature, end with a locking stitch and clip the thread; if your machine doesn't include this option, extend the length of your overlapped stitches to about ½" from your starting point.

Continue stitching.

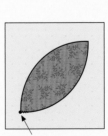

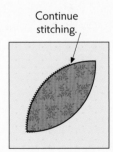

Stop and pivot.

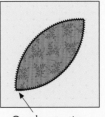

Overlap starting point slightly.

Pin Point Tip

LOCKING STITCH BENEFIT

When stitching my appliqué projects, I've trained myself to end each piece with a locking stitch, meaning that the machine takes a small handful of stitches in place to secure the seam. Locking stitches can be placed in the appliqué edge *or* in the background cloth, so my goal is to choose a position where the print of the cloth will disguise them best. The greatest benefit to the locking stitch is that it resets the sewing machine and brings the needle back to the starting position, making it easy to align each new appliqué under the needle for stitching.

4. For blocks with two or more appliqués spaced closely together, I recommend taking the "string appliqué" approach. This means that as the stitching of each appliqué is finished, instead of clipping the threads, lift the presser foot and slide the block background to the next appliqué without moving it from the sewing-machine surface. Continue stitching in this manner to complete the design, and then carefully clip the threads between the appliqués.

Removing Paper Pattern Pieces

1. From the wrong side of the block, use embroidery scissors to carefully pinch and cut through the cloth underneath the appliqué approximately ¼" from the stitched edge. Trim away the background fabric

underneath the appliqué, leaving a generous ¼" seam allowance inside the shape to keep it secure.

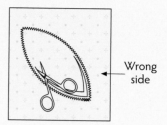

Wrong side

2. To remove the paper, grasp the appliqué edge between the thumb and finger of one hand, and grab the seam allowance immediately opposite with the other hand. Give a gentle but firm tug to free the paper edge from the line of stitching. Slide your fingertip between the paper and the appliqué to loosen the pattern piece where it's anchored to the cloth with glue stick and pull the paper straight out from the stitched seam as you work around the shape. Use tweezers with a rounded tip to remove any paper piece that might be stuck in a point or area of the seam, remembering that if it's too small to easily grab and remove, it's too small to worry about!

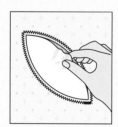

3. After all paper pattern pieces have been removed, lay the block wrong side up on the pressing surface and *briefly* press the seam allowances with a hot iron to ensure they're lying smooth and flat.

Quilting the Quilt

There are many options available for finishing your quilt. In-depth details for the choices, and the final steps needed to implement them, can be found at ShopMartingale.com/HowtoQuilt.

If you choose to have your quilt top finished with machine quilting, you'll want to be sure the seams have been pressed well and are lying flat and in the intended direction. Stay-stitching the patchwork around the perimeter of the top, about ⅛" in from the raw edge, is also a good idea—this takes just a few moments and is well worth the time because it will keep the seams along the quilt edge secure. Last, to preserve the seam allowances and prevent fraying while the top is handled, I suggest applying a thin line of liquid seam sealant along the raw edges.

CHUBBY BINDING

Complete step-by-step instructions for traditional binding can be found on the Martingale website as previously referenced. My more unconventional "chubby binding" features a single layer of binding that has a traditional look from the front and a wide width of binding on the back to beautifully frame your quilt backing and reduce bulk at the mitered corners. Here are the steps I use:

1. Cut the binding strips 2" wide (instead of the traditional 2½" width) as instructed in the project directions and join the strips end to end using straight (not diagonal) seams.

2. Using a bias-tape maker designed to produce 1"-wide double-fold tape, feed the binding strip through the tool *wrong side up* so the resulting folds of the strip are visible as you work. As the strip emerges from the

maker, press it flat with a hot iron so the raw folded edges meet at the center of the strip; this pressing step will automatically direct the seam allowances where the strip has been joined to one side, resting flat and in the same direction.

3. Open the pressed binding strip along the top edge only, turn the end under approximately ½" to hide the raw edge, and position it onto the quilt top at one side, not a corner. Pin and then stitch the binding in place along the first side of the quilt, stopping ¼" from the first corner, and take a few backstitches (or use a locking stitch).

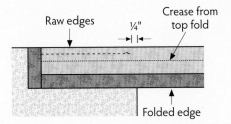

4. Make a fold in the binding, bringing it back down onto itself to square the corner, and then pin the remainder in place along the next side of the quilt. Rotate and position the corner of the quilt under the presser foot and stitch the next section of pinned binding. Continue in this manner to sew the binding to the entire quilt top, cutting the raw end about 1" beyond your starting point.

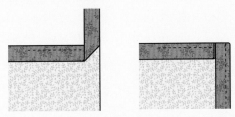

5. Bring the wide folded edge of the binding from the front of the quilt to the back, mitering the corners, and pin it in place. From the back of the quilt, use a needle and matching thread to hand sew a blind stitch along the binding edge and anchor it in place.

About the Author

In the late 1990s, Kim became a quilter almost by accident. While at a sidewalk sale one day she chanced upon some beautiful fabrics and a sampler quilt pattern that she couldn't pass by. With no one to mentor her or show her how to sew a quilt, Kim impulsively bought everything and worked her way through the steps one by one. By the completion of her quilt, she was hooked!

Shortly after finishing that first quilt, and not realizing how little she still knew, Kim entered a quilting contest hosted by *American Patchwork & Quilting* magazine. Amazingly, with just the third quilt she'd ever made, Kim won! This win gave her the courage to submit several designs to the magazine for consideration. Each of them was accepted, and with her fourth quilt Kim began publishing.

Designing for magazines led to a steady series of "Simple" books with Martingale & Company, published over the course of nearly 20 years. This, in turn, took Kim down a new path, and she traveled extensively for more than 10 years sharing her quilts and teaching her self-taught quiltmaking methods.

When given the chance to try her hand at fabric design for Henry Glass & Company, Kim jumped at the opportunity, bringing her quiltmaking journey full circle. Because it all started with the fabric! To date, she has more than 40 fabric collections under her belt in her signature scrap-basket style.

These days Kim stays closer to home, enjoying time with her husband, her two little granddaughters she's nicknamed Puddin' Cup and Sugar Pie, and her small pack of pups that includes two adopted rescue dogs. Her days are filled with gardening and cooking, quilting and designing, walking dogs and fifth wheeling, and life is good!